Evaluating Children's Writing

A Handbook of Communication Choices for Classroom Teachers

Evaluating Children's Writing

A Handbook of Communication Choices for Classroom Teachers

SUZANNE BRATCHER

Northern Arizona University

ST. MARTIN'S PRESS, New York

Editor: Naomi Silverman
Manager, publishing services: Emily Berleth
Publishing services associate: Kalea Chapman
Project management: Omega Publishing Services, Inc.
Art director: Sheree Goodman
Text design: Gene Crofts
Cover art: Eileen Burke
Additional artwork: Terri Robinson and Sandy Wright

Library of Congress Catalog Card Number: 92-63134
Manufactured in the United States of America.
87654
fedcba

For information, write:
St. Martin's Press, Inc.
175 Fifth Avenue
New York, NY 10010

ISBN: 0-312-08121-9

Acknowledgments

Figures 4.5, 4.6, 4.7, 4.8, 4.9, 4.10, and 4.16. From Arizona Student Assessment Program Scoring Guide for Writing, Poem, Form 3A, Assessment 5, page one, rubrics for observations one and two, and related anchor and training papers. Copyright 1993 by The Riverside Publishing Company. All rights reserved. No part of this work may be reproduced or transmitted in any form by any means, electronic or mechanical, including photocopying and recording, or by any information storage or retrieval system without the prior written permission of The Riverside Publishing Company unless such copying is expressly permitted by federal copyright law.

Figure 11.1. Graphic from *Write to Learn,* Second Edition by Donald M. Murray. Copyright © 1987, by Holt, Rinehart and Winston, Inc. Reproduced by permission of the publisher.

Dedicated to
    the teachers of
    the Northern Arizona Writing Project,
    who kept asking until I answered

PREFACE

What This Book Is

When the subject of evaluating children's writing comes up, teachers sometimes bristle, and when the word "grading" is introduced, some simply leave the room. *Evaluating Children's Writing* addresses this threatening—even painful—topic. It is about judging children's progress in writing, and it is about arriving at numbers or letters, checks and minuses, or smiling and frowning faces, whatever icons teachers use to communicate degrees of success (or failure) to students. *Evaluating Children's Writing* introduces and explains a wide range of evaluation strategies used by classroom teachers to arrive at grades. Samples of student writing accompany the instructions to illustrate the techniques. An appendix of additional student writing is provided for readers who wish to practice particular evaluation strategies.

But *Evaluating Children's Writing* is more than just a catalog of grading options; it is a handbook with a point of view. At the same time that it offers recipes for grading techniques, it also offers a philosophy of evaluating student writing that encourages teachers to put grading into a communication context and to analyze their own individual communication situations. It suggests making choices among the many options for evaluation by determining the instructional purpose of the assignment and considering the advantages and disadvantages of the particular strategy.

Who This Book Is For

This book is for teachers interested in exploring options for evaluating writing. It is for teachers who know how to grade one way but want to experiment with other methods. It is for teachers who are uncomfortable with the way they currently grade writing and for student teachers just learning to grade. It is for teachers who want to add writing to their repertoire of teaching tools but have been hesitant because they have wondered how to evaluate their students' work. While this handbook is primarily aimed at elementary teachers, the principles it lays out are appropriate to the evaluation of writing at any level; therefore, some secondary teachers may find it helpful as well.

The Purpose of This Book

This book is about evaluation—the process which individual teachers use to arrive at marks for their students. It is not about school-wide assessment of writing or about state or national writing assessment. While most elementary teachers are charged with teaching writing, very few teacher education programs include explicit instruction in grading writing. But evaluation is an important skill. Most schools require teachers to give grades, and society emphasizes fairness in grades. Instinctively, teachers know that writing is a complex process, a process that requires mastery of context, content, form, and language. However, evaluation is not instinctive.

Like most teachers of writing, I agree with Stephen and Susan Tchudi (1991), "In our ideal world, student writing and other composing would always be 'graded' pass/fail, successful/unsuccessful, or credit/no credit" (p. 155). Unfortunately, however, most of us do not inhabit "ideal world" schools. However much we might wish to evaluate our students' writing as "successful/ unsuccessful," we are literally forced to grade writing. Without explicit instruction in how to evaluate, most of us have taught ourselves to grade, haphazardly, often simply duplicating the way we were graded as students. As with many self-taught skills, learned by necessity rather than by design, evaluation is often a frustrating process for both teachers and students.

The purpose of this book is to offer specific grading strategies and explicit instructions for using them, to offer options so that we may be intentional about our grading rather than haphazard. *Evaluating Children's Writing* is meant to be used with a group—in an in-service or in a class—but it can also be used as a self-help, self-teaching handbook. It is meant to be used as a reference for step-by-step procedures of grading techniques that can be used at different times during the year. *Evaluating Children's Writing* offers suggestions about the craft of evaluation—guidelines for instructional objectives, for student audience analysis, and for teacher self-analysis that help define communication contexts. It also offers a catalog of techniques, options appropriate for a variety of classroom environments. The art of grading—the ability to address the nuances of particular situations by designing innovative hybrids—remains for the individual teacher to master with years of experience.

The Design of the Book

Evaluating Children's Writing is divided into three parts:

I. The Objectives of Evaluation
II. Evaluation Options
III. Using Evaluation as a Teaching Tool

Part I is designed to help teachers identify teaching objectives for the writing assignments they make. Part II enumerates evaluation options (approaches to grading, response strategies, management systems, evaluation styles) and provides specific instructions for implementing these options. Part III puts evaluation into a context larger than a single writing assignment. It raises questions about choosing from among the options and about using evaluation as a teaching tool. It suggests methods by which teachers may teach themselves to grade. Exercises throughout the book offer opportunities for practicing the different techniques, and the appendix provides samples of real student writing that may be used for practice.

Where This Book Came From

For the past several years I have directed a site of the National Writing Project at my university. During the school year I have worked with student teachers in a class we call "Writing to Learn." During the summers I have worked with public school teachers who have come to campus for a five-week Summer Institute. Both groups of teachers are enthusiastic about teaching writing, but at the end of our time together, they invariably say, "O.K. Now—how do I grade my students' writing?"

This handbook resulted from my work to answer that question. I discovered that there are many answers, and that each answer depends (as does writing itself) on the context.

The Bias of This Book

I have taught writing at many levels (sixth grade through graduate school), in many contexts for over twenty years; for fifteen or so of those years I was uncomfortable with grading. So every time a new "answer" to evaluation came down the pike, I jumped on the bandwagon, searching for the perfect grading technique. This search has been fraught with hope and frustration, and it has taught me a lot about writing, about evaluating writing, about my students, and about myself.

I believe that each of the evaluation methods included in this book has a place in teaching writing: they are all different; they all work; none of them is perfect. What we need as teachers of writing is intentionality in grading: we need a smorgasbord of grading strategies from which to choose. We need the ability to match grading techniques to teaching purposes. Grading is communication, and the "proper" grading strategy depends not on the winds of fad in the profession, but on the particular teaching purpose of the lesson or the unit or the course itself. Successful grading resides not in the particular grading strategy, but in the teacher's decision making, not in the requirements of the grading form, but in teaching purpose.

While I now teach writing from a strong process bias, I began teaching in 1971—before the paradigm shift occurred that Hairston described in 1982. Therefore, I retain a certain tolerance for a product bias as well. I believe that neither a process orientation nor a product orientation is sufficient by itself. Balance is required. (Indeed, the profession is leaning this way: "process toward product" is what we hear more and more.) Throughout this book, I refer to the "writing process," assuming that the reader knows this almost-jargon term. But in case this orientation toward writing is unfamiliar to some, let me explain what I mean by it. Very briefly, I mean the method that writers use to go from a blank sheet of paper to a finished written product. The writing process is recursive and messy, but when we pull out the themes that run through it for most writers, we find *prewriting* (gathering ideas, thinking, organizing), *drafting* (putting words into sentences and sentences into paragraphs), *revising* (rethinking ideas, adding, deleting), *editing* (correcting mechanics), and *publishing* (sharing the finished work with others).

But no matter the teaching bias, in order to evaluate writing with any degree of satisfaction, first we have to ask ourselves, "What is my instructional purpose for this assignment?" And then we have to ask not only which activity will accomplish the purpose, but also which grading strategy will best accomplish the purpose. By putting grading into a communication context, we can make it an extension of our teaching. After all, we came into this profession to be teachers, not to be graders.

Cautions to the Reader

Perhaps the biggest danger of writing a book about evaluation is that the very existence of the book will put too much emphasis on grading writing. John Harmon, in an article entitled "The Myth of Measurable Improvement," advises teachers not to evaluate on day-to-day growth. He asserts that growth in writing is slow and that evaluation is meaningless unless sufficient time has elapsed to allow for growth. He compares young writers to young plants: if we check their growth every day, we will surely be discouraged! I agree with Harmon. I intend the strategies in this book to be used after enough time has passed to allow for growth and *only when grades are necessary*. Not every piece of writing needs to be graded. In fact, when writing is used as a learning tool, it should probably not be graded. And even when students write for the purpose of learning to write, I do not believe that their efforts should be graded on every characteristic presented here. For example, not every piece of writing will be taken through all the stages of the writing process; many will stop after a first draft or even after prewriting. So, not every piece of writing should be graded as if it were a finished product. Further, I believe very strongly that emergent writers should not be graded at all; instead they should be encouraged to write more, to take ever-increasing risks in an environment safe from grades. I hope this book will be a tool for teachers to use in situations in which they find grades either useful or necessary. I hope it will not be used as a weapon to justify constant evaluation of children as they practice and learn the complex mode of communication we call "writing."

Acknowledgments

Like any writer, I could never have finished this task without the help and support of other people. I want to thank all of the teachers who helped me gather samples of student writing: Amy Caldwell, Cathy Capes, Marie Hammerle, Wanda Heronemus, Carmen Johnson, Jan Larson, Connie Miles, Dawn Reeves, Linda Ryan, and Bernie Whistler. I also want to thank the people who read my manuscript and made suggestions for its improvement: Connie Miles; at St. Martin's Press, my editor Naomi Silverman; and the reviewers who provided excellent suggestions and thoughtful criticism: Wendy Bishop, Florida State University; Nancy Hansen-Krening, University of Washington; Mary Heller, Kansas State University; Brenda H. Loyd, University of Virginia; Betty L. Rider, Delaware Hayes High School; Duane Roen, Syracuse University; and Tony Silva, Purdue University. And last I want to thank my family—Greg and Jane—for their encouragement and patience.

References Hairston, Maxine. "Thomas Kuhn and the Winds of Change," *College Composition and Communication*, 33, (1982), pp. 76–88.

Harmon, John. "The Myth of Measurable Improvement." *English Journal*, 77:5 (September, 1988), pp. 78–80.

Tchudi, Stephen and Susan Tchudi. *The English/Language Arts Handbook: Classroom Strategies for Teachers.* Portsmouth, NH: Heinemann, 1991.

CONTENTS

Evaluating Children's Writing

*A Handbook of
Communication Choices
for Classroom Teachers*

PART I

The Objectives of Evaluation

Part I explores grading as an act of communication between teacher and students. First, our feelings about grading set the stage for this instructional communication. Second, the many different instructional settings in which we find ourselves drive the decisions we make about how to teach our students. Third, the pieces of the grading puzzle (context, content, structure, mechanics, and process) provide a wide variety of purposes for the writing assignments we make. The theme of this part is that evaluation should serve instruction, not vice versa.

1

Mechanics
Definition
Grade-level Applications and Examples
Process
Definition
Applications and Examples

CHAPTER 1

In the Background
How We Feel about Grading

Just after Christmas I was walking down the hall in a K–6 elementary school. On the stairway I encountered a friend, a fourth grade teacher.

I said, "Hi, Ellen [not her real name, of course]. How are you today?"

She groaned. "It's almost report card time! Do you really need to ask?"

I shrugged with what I hoped was the appropriate amount of sympathy.

"You know," she went on in an agonized voice, "I don't know why I leave grading papers till the last minute." She looked at me as if I might be able to enlighten her.

I shrugged sympathetically again.

"It's just that I feel so guilty about grading," she rushed on. "I know grades are important," she added defensively. "I know parents and kids need to know how they're doing, but. . . ." Her voice trailed off.

"Yes, . . ." I began.

"It's just that I work so hard to build a relationship of encouragement and trust with my children in their writing." Her tone was plaintive, the grieving tone of an adult when a favorite dog has died. "And then suddenly I have to become judge and jury." She looked off down the empty hall and spoke more to herself than to me. "Almost every one of my kids tries hard at writing. I just hate to discourage the late bloomers, the slow little turtles who will likely win the race one day."

She turned and looked at me, as if suddenly remembering my presence. "You know what I mean?" she asked.

I nodded. "Yes, . . ." I said, ready to offer my heartfelt condolences. But she had turned down the hall toward her room.

I stood watching her go, her question echoing in my ears: "Why do I leave my grading to the last minute?" Why indeed?

As teachers of writing, we all know exactly how Ellen was feeling that day. We struggle with the dichotomy of teacher versus grader whenever we take up student writing, not just when report cards are due to go home. In fact, we

3

often wind up feeling positively schizophrenic. As Ellen said, we work hard to earn our students' trust as we try to help them improve their writing. We instinctively know the truth of Donald Murray's assertion: "The writing teacher must not be a judge, but a physician. His job is not to punish, but to heal" (Lindemann, 1987, p. 191).

But we must grade student writing.

A review of recent books on the subject of teaching writing emphasizes the schizophrenia we feel when we stare at a stack of papers, grade book open. Most of the literature rejects even the word "grading." Instead writers use words like "assessing," "evaluating," "responding." We read the books, and we agree. But most schools still demand grades. Linda Cleary sums up the conflict we find ourselves in. "Grades," she says, "are a subject that educators tend to avoid; they are as connected with the American Way as mother, apple pie, and grammar" (p. 156).

No wonder Ellen puts off grading her students' writing. She enjoys reading what they have written. It's easy to respond, to reply to what her students have said, even to make suggestions for future writing. It's not so easy to put a grade on the paper, to reduce the comments she has made to a "B," to a "+," or to an "S."

And when the literature addresses "assessment" or "evaluation," writers talk about teaching students to assess their own writing or about teacher response to student writing in a conference setting (Anson, 1989). Most often, what discussions we do find about grading in the literature are apologetic, beginning something like this: "First, let us suggest some general principles about grading. 1. Grading should be deemphasized" (Kirby and Liner, 1988).

Again, we can understand Ellen's frustration. She agrees with Kirby and Liner. She wants to deemphasize grading. She talks to her students about writing as a process, a process of getting better. She has explained that the individual grade is not important; progress is the important thing. She has told parents the same things on Back-to-School Night. Still, she watches Billy wad up his paper angrily and throw it in the trash can after she returns it. She knows it's the "C" he resents, possibly because his classmates have told him that a "C" is "terrible," possibly because his father does not pay him for "Cs." In any case, he is responding to the grade, not to her written comment—"I wish I could visit your grandma's farm"—at the end of the paper. And she knows that Sally, a little girl who sits next to Billy, never takes her papers home at all. Ellen realizes that these students would respond differently if she'd put only the comments on the papers.

The books don't say much to Ellen about how to put a letter or a number on a paper. They don't say much about how to translate a group of those letters or numbers into a grade that can be written on a report card or entered into a computer. Instead, writers of books about teaching writing tell us that students should be evaluated only against their own progress—comparing writing facility at the beginning of the year to writing facility at the end of the year (Goodman, Goodman, and Hoods, eds. 1989, p. 78). Furthermore, the literature warns us to always be positive, to use grades to encourage students, not to hinder them (Schwartz, 1991, pp. 122–123; Graves, 1983, p. 93). And Cleary goes even further, "in analyzing . . . forty students' experience with writing, I came to this conclusion: *It isn't productive to connect writing with grades* [her italics]" (Cleary, 1991, p. 156). Frank Smith agrees. "Grading never taught a writer anything," he says (1988, p. 30).

Ellen knows all of this. She has seen it in her classroom, and not just in Billy and Sally. Anna, the best writer in the class, the student who always receives "As," writes at the end of the year exactly like she did the first week of school. So Ellen finds herself putting off grading until the last minute. She reads her students' writing eagerly and enjoys writing responses to what they've written, but she is reluctant to put grades on the papers. She enjoys telling Billy she likes his description of his dog and wants to know more about the day he got it, but she finds herself avoiding the label of a grade. She wants to help Billy feel good about his writing; she doesn't want to discourage him with a grade. Ellen's distress over grading has become so severe that sometimes she takes her students' papers home and leaves them there until she is forced to put grades on them—when she faces a stack of new papers to grade or a blank report card that must be filled in.

Many of us feel as Ellen does. In the struggle to change teaching practices over the last ten or fifteen years, we have begun to see writing differently, to see our students differently. We have lived through and been part of the paradigm shift Maxine Hairston (1982) described. We no longer emphasize the products of writing to the exclusion of the process. We no longer assign writing in isolation.

We take students through prewriting activities to build background and to help them learn to think through what they know and what they need to find out in order to write thoughtful prose. We help them visualize different audiences and different purposes. Ellen, for example, spent the better part of two language arts periods simply reading examples of personal narratives to her students before they began to write one themselves.

We take our students through drafting to help them separate composing from editing, ideas from surface considerations. Another teacher friend of mine, Sarah, tells me she spends two weeks of language arts time taking her students through multiple work sessions on drafts of any paper they will publish to parents.

We walk students through revising to help them understand that writing is fluid, not fixed, that it can always be improved, that other people participate in writing with us. Sarah has divided her students into "writing pods," groups of four students who read each other's writing and make comments based on a content rubric of criteria she develops with the class for each assignment (another couple of language arts periods).

We work with students on editing to help them become proficient at controlling grammar and usage. We suggest strategies for helping each other with the surface correctness requirements of written language. After the students have revised their writing for the ideas and content, Sarah's pods next divide up the tasks of editing among themselves, choosing to examine each other's papers for punctuation errors, or spelling errors, or capitalization errors (yet another language arts period).

We provide publishing opportunities. We celebrate the product of all the hard work that has gone before. Ellen has an author's chair, where students sit to read their work aloud to the class. Sarah has publishing parties, complete with cookies.

We take up the papers. We read them and feel good about the writing our students have done.

And then we must grade those papers.

Parents, principals, school boards, cumulative records, junior high counselors—all demand that we grade student writing. Most of our students have taken us at our word. They have participated in prewriting, in drafting, in revising, in editing: they have followed the process. And yet there are differences in what they have been able to produce. As teachers we know that writing is not exact, that we are not striving for perfection either in our own writing or in our students' writing. As graders "A+" represents the perfect paper—the one that is error free. Teacher/grader schizophrenia settles upon us.

Finally, because we know we must, we take pen in hand and grade, feeling like the student teacher who said to me one day, "I feel so bad putting all those red marks on my students' hard work. It really does look like I bled all over their papers." Trying to avoid this unfortunate metaphor, we have sometimes graded in blue, bleeding like an aristocrat, or in green, like a snake.

There is hope, however. Teacher/grader schizophrenia can be overcome. If we choose a grading option that matches our teaching purposes, we do not need to bleed at all. And neither do our students.

Chapter Summary

Most of us suffer from "teacher/grader schizophrenia." On the one hand, we are committed to teaching writing as a process. We have read the research on learning to write and understand the rationale for being positive in our response to our students' writing. On the other hand, we are locked into school situations that require us to translate our response to our students' writing into letter grades or even numbers. But there is hope: teacher/grader schizophrenia can be overcome by choosing grading options that match our teaching purposes.

EXERCISES

1. Remember when you were an elementary student. Who was your favorite teacher? Why? How did he or she grade your work? Who was your least favorite teacher? How did he or she grade your work?

2. Write a brief "writing autobiography." Write about when you first started to write and how you developed through school as a writer. What were your feelings about yourself as a writer at different stages in your "writing life"? Were these feelings related to the grades you got in school? Why or why not?

3. Plot yourself on the following "feelings about grading" continuum. Explain why you placed yourself where you did.

|------------------------------------|------------------------------------|

I think about
quitting my job
when I have to
grade papers.

I have no feelings
about grading—I
don't care one way
or the other.

I look forward
to grading.

References   Anson, Chris, ed. *Writing and Response: Theory, Practice, and Research.* Urbana, IL: National Council of Teachers of English, 1989.

Cleary, Linda Miller. *From the Other Side of the Desk: Students Speak Out About Writing.* Portsmouth, NH: Heinemann, 1991.

Goodman, Kenneth, Yetta Goodman and Wendy Hood, eds. *The Whole Language Evaluation Book.* Portsmouth, NH: Heinemann, 1989.

Graves, Donald. *Writing: Teachers and Children at Work.* Portsmouth, NH: Heinemann, 1983.

Hairston, Maxine. "Thomas Kuhn and the Winds of Change," *College Composition and Communication, 33* (1982), pp. 76–88.

Kirby, Dan and Tom Liner. *Inside Out: Developmental Strategies for Teaching Writing,* 2nd ed. Portsmouth, NH: Heinemann, 1988.

Lindemann, Ericka. *A Rhetoric for Writing Teachers,* 2nd ed. New York: Oxford University Press, 1987.

Schwartz, Mimi, ed. *Writer's Craft, Teacher's Art: Teaching What We Know.* Portsmouth, NH: Heinemann, 1991.

Smith, Frank. *Joining the Literacy Club.* Portsmouth, NH: Heinemann, 1988.

CHAPTER 2

Specific Situations
Putting Evaluation into a Context

Definition: Grading—Communication between teacher and student that is designed to enhance the student's writing.

Using the above definition of grading to discuss the context of grading—specific evaluation situations—leads us to a familiar schematic called "the communication triangle." This triangle can help us articulate the various contexts in which we grade. Often the teacher/grader schizophrenia we suffer results from our having unconsciously created grading contexts that are at odds with our carefully constructed teaching contexts. Let's look at the communication triangle as it can be applied to evaluation.

The communication triangle has three equally important considerations: the audience intended to receive the communication, the purpose of the communication, and the stance (or chosen attitude) of the communicator. Adapting this triangle to our purposes, we label the three corners "student," "teacher," and "instructional purpose," as illustrated in Figure 2.1.

Moving around the triangle as we usually encounter it, we find the following corners: the official purpose of evaluation is to collect data over time that will allow us to justify nine-week grades for the report card; the teacher stance is that of judge, trying to fairly and accurately determine quality of student work; student needs and expectations are implicit at best and often never really thought through at all. (Students who do the best job inferring the criteria the teacher considers important for the report card are the ones who receive "As.")

In this traditional grading situation, the communication triangle has one very important corner—the purpose corner. That corner dictates a second

FIGURE 2.1. Communication Triangle

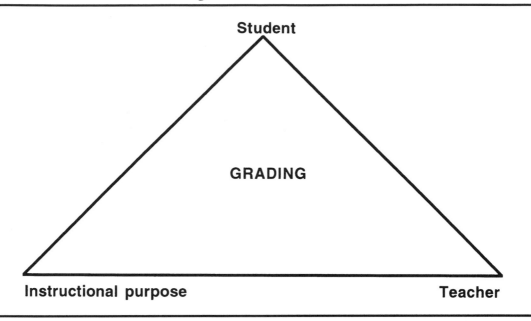

corner—the teacher corner—and the third corner, the student corner, is almost nonexistent. Grading communication winds up looking more like a line than a triangle:

Purpose   Teacher (Student)

The end product of this lopsided triangle is very poor communication at grading time and lots of unhappy feelings for both teachers and students. To control the context in which our grading takes place, we must make that context explicit—for ourselves and for our students. We need to analyze each corner of the grading/communication triangle carefully.

Student Audience Considerations

When we write, we picture the readers to whom we are writing—we analyze the audience and attempt to communicate with them. When we evaluate or grade, we should do the same thing. Perhaps the central challenge of teaching is getting to know a particular set of students, finding out what they already know, and determining how to bridge the gap between where they are and where we want them to arrive. This challenge becomes most obvious when we try to grade a piece of writing (or a nine-week pattern of writing).

The question of how to interpret a particular effort from an individual student can be answered in an intentional way if student (audience) analysis is formally carried out by the teacher. The questions that follow (as well as others) can be used to inform grading and make it an extension of, rather than something separate from, teaching.

Sample Student Audience Analysis
a. What do my students already know about writing?
b. What do they like about writing?
c. What do they dislike about writing?
d. What do I think they need to learn next?

Let's take an example of a fourth grade class in a small town. The teacher, Mrs. Johnson, hands out a writing inventory at the beginning of the year to discover the attitudes her students have toward writing. As she plans her writing instruction, she wants to establish comfort with writing first, before moving on to confidence and finally competence. She asks five questions:

Do you like to write? (Students check either "I love to write," "I like to write sometimes," "I only write when I have to," or "I hate to write.")
Do you think you are a good writer?
What have you written recently?
What kinds of things do you like to write about?
How do you think learning to write better will help you?

Then she has them complete the sentence "I think that writing is . . ." (adapted from Bratcher and Larson, 1992).

From this questionnaire, Mrs. Johnson discovers several things about her student audience:

First, she discovers that almost 75 percent of her students like to write, at least some of the time. The other 25 percent, however, strongly dislike writing. And, she discovers an interesting match between how the students feel about writing and whether or not they consider themselves good writers: in her class there is an 88 percent correlation between students liking to write and considering themselves good writers!

Second, she discovers that the vast majority of the writing her students do is school-related. The few students who write on their own outside of school seem to write stories, poems, and letters.

Third, she discovers that for almost 75 percent of her students there is a large discrepancy between what they are actually writing in school and what they like to write about. The most popular topics among her class are animals, family, and friends. The most popular form is fiction.

Fourth, Mrs. Johnson discovers that almost half of her students view learning to write better as a tool for school and later work. Almost a third of her students do not see learning to write better as something that will help them at all.

Finally, from the sentence completion, Mrs. Johnson learns that about half of her class views writing as fun sometimes.

Mrs. Johnson now has a pretty good picture of her students' attitudes about writing. From her analysis she has learned that she is fortunate because a large number of the children in her class have good feelings about themselves as writers. But she has also learned that she needs to work with some of her students on how they view themselves as writers. Beyond that, she has learned some topics that her students might like to write on. Further, she has learned that the class as a whole needs to expand its understanding of why writing well will help them in their lives.

She can now begin designing her writing instruction for this class. A large number of the students are comfortable, even confident, about their writing and can be challenged toward greater and greater competence. But some of the students are not yet comfortable with writing; they don't even see its importance. Mrs. Johnson decides to begin with cooperative groups, groups that contain confident students as well as uncomfortable students, hoping to use the confident students as encouragers and leaders for the others.

Later in the year, Mrs. Johnson will do more specific audience analyses on specific criteria. For example, when she first teaches editing, she will locate the expert spellers as well as the terrible spellers. She can then offer peer support as well as specialized instruction to the poor spellers.

Instructional Purposes of Grading

Most of us become frustrated with evaluation because we resent what it does to our teaching. Cleary says: "Most teachers see grading as a stumbling block to what they wish they could do differently" (p. 156). Students focus (very pragmatically) on the grades we assign to their writing and seem to ignore our efforts to help them improve. This attitude is especially obvious among students at the extreme ends of the grading scale—the "E" students and the "N" students. How often do we see progress or change in these two populations? They seem to come to us as "E" writers or "N" writers and stay that way as long as they are in our classrooms: the "E" writers are as static and unchanging, as unlearning, as are the "N" writers. Even among the middle population, though, the change is often slight. When was the last time an "S" writer in one of your classes became an "E" writer by the end of the year?

But all of that can change in a classroom where evaluation is seen as a communication tool rather than as a record-keeping function. When grading criteria are made to serve instruction (and therefore change as the teaching emphasis changes), students must focus on the objectives of the writing instruction to get the grades they want.

On a theoretical level it sounds easy, but on a practical level this approach changes writing instruction as well as evaluation. If student grades are to reflect levels of accomplishment of instructional purpose(s), we must first have a clear grasp of the teaching purpose of any given assignment. Evaluation criteria then grow naturally from the instructional purpose(s) of the assignment. So, grading purpose(s) begins with assignment creation.

The list of possible teaching purposes for writing assignments is infinite. But perhaps a list of a few with possible assignments that accompany them will illustrate:

Demonstrate the Writing Process

Sample assignment: Turn in every scrap of paper that went into writing your personal narrative. Be sure to turn in your mind map, your rough draft, your response sheet from your writing group, your editing workshop checklist, and your final draft.

Communicate with a Specific Audience

Sample assignment: Write a Valentine's Day story for Mr. Cook's first-grade class using the vocabulary words he supplied us with.

Demonstrate Mastery of Specific Content

Sample assignment: Write an interview between yourself and Charles Wallace (*A Wind in the Door,* by Madeleine L'Engle).

Discover New Content

Sample assignment: Write a biography of your favorite author (Shel Silverstein, Dr. Seuss, Louisa May Alcott, etc.).

Of course any one writing assignment may (and probably will) have more than one teaching objective, but it is important that the teacher clearly delineate both the primary and secondary objectives. Thus, the purpose of evaluation changes from a record-keeping function to a teaching function: evaluating how well the piece of writing accomplishes its stated purpose(s). Specific criteria and explanations of the grade point out to the student how the writing could more effectively accomplish its purpose. Coupled with an opportunity for revision or with a follow-up assignment, the graded writing becomes not an ending point but a starting point for the student. Learning becomes more effective because it is focused and goal-driven. To illustrate, let's look at a second-grade class late in the year.

Miss Wells asks her students to write a personal narrative, a story about something that happened to them that they want to remember. She has four possible teaching purposes for this assignment. She wants her students to:

1. choose a topic that interests their readers (the class).
2. tell a story using themselves as narrators.
3. use details in their writing.
4. edit for capitalization, complete sentences, and spelling.

Miss Wells then identifies her primary teaching purpose(s) as well as her secondary purposes. She proceeds to tailor instruction appropriate to her emphasis at the moment. Following instruction, a student in her class, John, turns in the following personal narrative shown in Figure 2.2.

Miss Wells must grade his paper. In her school, primary students are given the following grades: (+)= beyond teacher expectations; (✓)= meets expectations; and (−)= below teacher expectations. Occasionally Miss Wells uses a (✓+) to indicate writing that is beyond her expectations in some areas, but at her expectation level in others.

Depending on the emphasis Miss Wells has made on the teaching purposes—which ones she has identified for herself and the class as primary teaching purpose(s) and secondary teaching purpose(s)—this same student paper may receive different grades.

For example, if Miss Wells has made this personal narrative assignment primarily a learning-to-write assignment, she may have identified teaching purposes number 1 (choose a topic that interests the readers) and number 3 (use details) as her primary teaching purposes. Her audience analysis may have shown that the class has had little practice in considering readers when they write. She has spent time with the class discussing what the other children might like to read and how to pick a topic from their journals.

In this context, John's paper will likely receive a "+." Very few of the children in the class have ever ridden a horse, and all of them would like to. John has included lots of details for a second-grader: he has told where he rode the horse, the name of his favorite horse, and a particular ride he went on. The personal narrative exceeds Miss Wells' expectations for audience awareness and details.

If, on the other hand, Miss Wells has made this writing assignment a concluding activity for a language/mechanics lesson, she may have identified teaching purpose number 4 (edit for capitalization, complete sentences, and spelling) as her primary purpose for this writing assignment. In this situation, her audience analysis has indicated that capitalization is the major new material; these rules are the ones that have been targeted in instruction.

In this context, John's paper will likely receive a (✓+). John's sentences are complete and his spelling is good, but he has misused capital letters in "a

FIGURE 2.2. John's Personal Narrative

My First Horse Ride

I went to Smoke Tree Ranch in Palm Springs, California. There I learned to ride a horse. It was a lot of fun.

One day my cousins and I even went on a Breakfast Ride.

My favorite horse to ride was Sarly.

The End

Breakfast Ride." His writing is beyond her expectations in spelling and complete sentences, but not at her expectations in use of capital letters.

Teacher Stance toward Grading

But what about the third corner of the triangle, the teacher corner? Sometimes (perhaps often) teachers feel at odds with evaluation. As mentioned before, this teacher/grader schizophrenia often results when we adopt a grading stance or persona that is at odds with our teaching persona. For example, as teachers we know that positive reinforcement has more power than negative, and we adopt a cheerleading persona. But as graders we often think we should be perfectionists, sticklers for detail, focused on the quality of the product offered for evaluation, and we adopt a judge-and-jury persona. In short, having given up hitting students with rulers generations ago, we are uncomfortable striking them with grading pens.

But with purpose-driven evaluation, we can grade with the same persona with which we teach. Students can be encouraged by knowing which criteria they met successfully and by having concrete suggestions about how to improve the criteria that were not met so successfully. The teacher can encourage and praise what is done well, separating it from what needs more work.

Further, with a match between teaching emphasis and evaluation criteria, the teacher can adjust later revisions and assignments to meet student needs illustrated by criteria not met by large numbers of students in the class. After a particular assignment has been graded, class discussions can focus on the same emphases instruction has focused on, serving as review and further challenge for students who need to relearn. Grading criteria can be tailored to assignments as students move to more complex writing.

To return to the example of Miss Wells. As a writing teacher, she has adopted the instructional stance of encourager. She wants her students to take risks with their writing, to stretch beyond what they can already do and move into new territory. Consequently, as a grader she wants to maintain this encouraging stance. In the first instance (the assignment was used as an audience-awareness task) Miss Wells will follow the "+" grade with an encouraging note to John. She may say something like this: "John, the class really enjoyed your personal narrative. What a good topic choice you made! I'd like to go to Smoke Tree Ranch and meet Sarly myself." She may comment to John orally about the capitalization error or she may let it go entirely.

As a language/mechanics teacher, Miss Wells has adopted a rather matter-of-fact, be-sure-to-brush-your-teeth, stance. As a grader of mechanical assignments, then, her stance will follow suit. In the second instance (the assignment was a follow-up to a language/mechanics lesson), her comments that follow the (✓+) may be like this: "John, you did a great job making all of your sentences complete. Your spelling is perfect in this paper as well—good job! In the second paragraph "a Breakfast Ride" does not need to be capitalized. Can you find the rule about that on our chart and point it out to me?"

In short, depending on her audience analysis, her instructional goals, and the stance she has taken as a teacher, Miss Wells' grade and response to a particular piece of writing may differ. In this context, there is no such thing as the perfect "+" paper. The grade a paper receives is determined by how well it meets the instructional goals Miss Wells has set for that particular assignment.

Let's examine another example: a TV news report. It is turned in by a sixth-grader, Karl, in Mr. Thayer's class (see Figure 2.3).

Context 1: The assignment is a part of a careers' unit. Following a field trip to the local TV station, Mr. Thayer asks each student to write a portion of a newscast for a class videotape. Karl is assigned to do a news' report on safety issues for children. Mr. Thayer's primary purpose (stated to his students) is to illustrate what news people do.

In this context, Karl would likely receive an excellent grade on the assignment. The writing shows a clear understanding of how a news report would sound. The mechanical errors are unimportant because this piece is meant to be read aloud by Karl to the video camera, and Karl knows what his own punctuation means.

Context 2: The assignment is a book report. Mr. Thayer has encouraged students to use creative formats, like a TV news' report or a journal entry or a letter between characters in the book, but the primary (stated) purpose of the assignment is to illustrate knowledge of the book. The book reports will be assembled in a class collection and kept for students to browse through when

FIGURE 2.3. Karl's Writing

Jimmy Jet

```
    This is News Channel 3 with Heidi Fogalson, Heidi thanks Bob.  Today
a 9 year old child in New Jersey was said to be turned into a t.v.
set. Yes I did say t.v.  He watched to much t.v., so he finally turned
into one. He watched it night and day.  He watched the news, t.v.
shows, soap operas, and cartoons.  He cherished the t.v.  The first
word he said was "t.v."  The first sentence was "change the channel
mom!"  He walked at five months old, so he could turn the t.v. knob.
So children, unless you want to be run on electricity, don't watch to
much t.v.  There's an old saying you are what you eat, well this boy
turned into what he watched.  That's all the news right now, thanks
for watching five "o" clock news.  Good-night.
```

---

they are choosing their next book. A secondary purpose is to illustrate editing skills—in particular compound sentences and homophones.

In this context, Karl would likely receive an unsatisfactory grade. First, "Jimmy Jet and his TV Set" is only one poem in a large collection of Shel Silverstein's, so the piece does not illustrate knowledge of the book's entirety. Second, the editing is extremely weak: the paper contains three run-on sentences (incorrectly handled compounds) and two misspellings of the homophone "too." Karl needs to rewrite, attending to the purposes of the assignment and the instruction he has received.

Chapter Summary

Although we do not generally think of it this way, grading is first and foremost communication between teacher and student. It is communication aimed at learning: it is a teaching tool. Evaluation can be far more effective communication if we explicitly respond to the considerations delineated by the communication triangle—the particular student audience we are working with, the purpose(s) of writing assignments, and our stance as teachers when we grade.

When evaluation is looked at in this way (as communication), it becomes clear that there are no hard-and-fast "correct" answers to grading. Rather, there are objectives to be articulated and options to choose from. Consideration of the communication triangle makes choices explicit and gives us the control to match our grading personae with our teaching personae.

EXERCISES

1. For a class you currently teach (or, for student teachers, one you can spend some time observing), do a grading analysis based on the communication triangle for one writing assignment:

   Writing Assignment (Report the instructions the student received here):

   Student Audience (What background do the students have for this assignment?)

   Purpose(s) of the Assignment:

   Primary:

   Secondary:

   Teacher Stance:

   a. What kind of teaching persona do I (or the teacher) use in this class?

> **b.** How can the teaching stance be translated into a grading persona for this assignment?

Grading Criteria:

After considering the three corners of the communication triangle, generate three grading criteria for this assignment. Weight them by percentage of the grade.

2. Choose a sample student paper from the appendix. Grade it twice—according to the two scenarios set for either Miss Wells' class or Mr. Thayer's class. If possible, grade the paper a third time according to the context you invented in Exercise 1.

References   Bratcher, Suzanne and Jan Larson. "Teaching the Personal Narrative: A Case Study in the Fourth Grade." Flagstaff, AZ: Unpublished essay, Spring 1992.

CHAPTER 3

The Pieces of the Grading Puzzle

To escape teaching/grading schizophrenia, we must delineate for ourselves the objectives we have for student writing. This task is daunting, to say the least, for (in a language arts context) we must take into account context, content, structure, and mechanics, as well as process. (In a social studies context, we may focus only on content.) Perhaps our writing puzzle, then, might look something like Figure 3.1. But how to grade for all the pieces of the writing puzzle?

When I sit down to work a puzzle, the first thing I do is sort the pieces by color. Next I study the picture on the box and decide where the blue pieces will go, where the green ones, and so on. As I begin to piece the puzzle together, I look closely at shades of color and shapes, differentiating a blue piece that is part of the sky from a blue piece that is part of the lake. In this chapter, grading is a picture puzzle; objectives of grading are the pieces. Hence, this chapter discusses each objective as if it were a truly discrete entity, but only for purposes of analysis and definition. It is important to remember, however, that in real writing the objectives discussed here impact one another and do not function as discrete entities. (For example, purpose often determines audience and audience often determines grammatical, or mechanical, choices.)

When you begin a puzzle, any order you bring to the task is arbitrary. So let's pick up the pieces one at a time and examine them. And just as we sometimes pick up a puzzle piece and examine it quickly, or indeed, leave it on the table and not look at it at all, readers should pick and choose among the definitions that follow, studying those that are unfamiliar and skipping others. The order I have chosen is: context, content, structure, mechanics, process.

Note: Particular grade-appropriate requirements referenced in this chapter are based on *Language Arts Essential Skills,* a listing of grade-appropriate writing behaviors provided by the Education Department of the state of Arizona. These writing behaviors are not intended as rigid standards; instead they are offered as representative guidelines. Furthermore, these behaviors overlap from year to year and cannot be isolated as appropriate for a single grade level. Readers should examine the listing provided by their own state departments of education or individual school district curriculum guides and adapt the principles in this chapter accordingly.

FIGURE 3.1. The Pieces of the Writing Puzzle

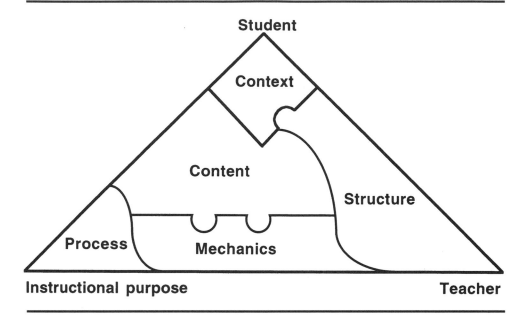

This chapter is provided primarily as a reference to commonly used terms; like a dictionary, it is not intended to be read paragraph by paragraph from beginning to end. Each section begins with a definition. The definition is followed by specific applications appropriate for particular grade-levels and examples of student writing.

Context

Definition

Context is the situation that creates and controls writing: reader, purpose, and writer's stance.

The *reader* for a student's writing may be a parent, a teacher, a friend, or simply the student himself or herself. Sometimes, of course, there may be more than one reader: the stated reader may be a class speaker (a thank-you letter, for example), but the teacher may be a reader as well if the letter will be evaluated before it is sent.

In any case, who the reader will be makes a tremendous difference to how the writing will be handled. A note to a friend, for example, can be written on scratch paper in pencil or crayon; spelling does not matter. A story the same student enters in a contest must conform to the requirements of the contest: it will need to be neat, and grammar will need to be accurate. It may even have to be written on special paper in ink, or perhaps it will need to be typed.

Likewise, the *purpose* for which the writer is writing will dictate certain decisions about the writing. A letter from a student to a parent asking for money to take on a field trip will need to be more complete in its explanation than a letter thanking the parent for the money after the trip is over. By the same token, a book report intended to prove that the student has read the entire book will require more detail than a book talk intended to entice another student to read the book.

The third part of the context of the writing that controls decision making is the *stance* of the writer, his or her voice in relationship to the audience and/or the content of the writing. In the first example above, if the child who is writing the request for money to take on the field trip has a parent who has plenty of money and is free with it, the letter may be cursory—an informative note. However, if the child has a parent who is either seriously short of money at the time or who is tightfisted, the letter may be petitionary—exhaustive in its defense of the need for the money.

In the book report example used above, if the student liked the book, the book report will be enthusiastic, even expansive in tone; it may even be longer than required by the teacher. If, however, the student disliked the book, the book report will be detached in tone and very likely as brief as possible.

Grade-level Applications and Examples

For students in grades K–3, the important components of context are the ability to identify the purpose of the writing and the student's personal satisfaction with his or her writing. The piece in Figure 3.2 (written by a third-grader) illustrates the ability to identify the purpose of writing. First the class read a story about an injured owl. This piece was then written in response to the assignment: "Would you be glad to be free if you were Little Red? Why or why not?"

Clearly, this student understands the purpose of this writing. The first sentence answers the question, even using some of the same words used in the prompt. (This sentence does, however, make it clear that the student does not consider the question to be as straightforward as perhaps the teacher does.) The next sentence goes on to answer the "Why?" by telling what the writer would do first upon gaining freedom.

In grades 4–6, it is important that students go further with context. They should learn to identify the reader(s) for their writing, as well as the purpose. At this level they can also begin to articulate their stance as writer to both the

FIGURE 3.2. Purpose

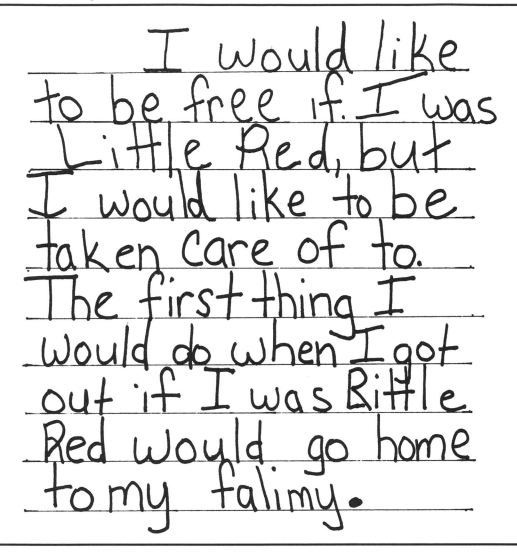

I would like to be free if. I was Little Red, but I would like to be taken care of to. The first thing I would do when I got out if I was Rittle Red would go home to my falimy.

reader(s) and the topic. The piece in Figure 3.3 (written by a fourth-grader) illustrates what happens when no reader has been identified for writing.

The writing in this piece is vague in the extreme. No names are included; no examples are cited. Had this writer been writing to a real audience, say to her mother, she would have felt safe to tell the story of what happened with "Jan" on the playground that afternoon. As it stands, the writer seems to have had no one at all in mind when she composed this piece.

FIGURE 3.3. No Reader

When you meet a new friend they are nice and kind. And then after you have played with her alot then she may get mean but they may stay nice and kind to you. They may start to be mean and angey at you then you get in a fight with her. You may not talk to each other but after a while you and her may be nice and say your sorry. Then you will be friends and she and you will probably meet new friends you and her will still stay friends but you may not. Then you and your new friend will be nice and kind to each other.

Content

Definition

Content consists of the ideas a writer uses. It takes in main idea articulation, use of details, and completeness of communication about ideas and/or events being discussed in the writing.

Content concerns cannot be taken for granted with elementary students. *Main idea* is a high-level thinking skill calling for synthesis of details. Because finding the main idea may seem intuitive to us as adults, teaching students to articulate the purpose or theme of what they are writing is sometimes difficult. Students often need lots of practice finding and expressing main ideas. Fred, telling the story of a nature walk, may list every stop along the way, even describe the stops in great detail, but may never write that the purpose of the walk was to find frogs.

Adding *details* can be difficult for students as well. Leah may write that she and her brother caught a bird and tried to give it a bath. She may consider this piece of writing funny without ever telling what the bird did when dunked in the bowl of water.

Students also frequently need help in making their stories *complete:* kids often believe that other people (especially adults) can read their minds, thus eliminating the necessity for explanation. In the example above, it may never occur to Leah that her readers might need to be told why the bird needed a bath in the first place. At the same time, kids sometimes don't realize that their readers have not had the same background experiences that they have had. If Julio is telling the story of his trip to New York City to his class in Billings, Montana, he may not realize he needs to explain what a subway is.

Grade-level Applications and Examples

In grades K–3, content concerns usually include completion of ideas and elimination of gaps or omissions that may be confusing to a reader without the same level of understanding about the topic as the student writer. Furthermore, teachers often begin to challenge students at this level to include details that support and explain the main idea of the writing. Figure 3.4 (written by a third grader) illustrates what happens when a student does not complete the idea. The assignment was "Do you think this story really happened or do you think it's make-believe? Why?"

The student clearly understands the purpose of the writing. He answers the first question, "Yes, I think it was real." He also knows he is supposed to tell

FIGURE 3.4. Completion of Ideas

why: he says "because," but he does not complete his thought. A reader will never know what the "because" meant to the writer, what his reasons were for coming to the conclusion that the story was not make-believe.

In grades 4–6, students are ready to learn to narrow a topic or a subject, to delineate the boundaries of the discussion or of the story. Juanita, for example, can choose to write only about what her family saw at the zoo, leaving out exhaustive descriptions of the 150 mile car trip that took them to the zoo and the explanation of her aunt's wedding that took them to Phoenix in the first place.

Beyond simply avoiding assumptions about a reader's knowledge, or gaps or omissions that interfere with a reader's understanding, students can begin to develop ideas with details tailored to the main idea of the piece of writing they are working on. The piece in Figure 3.5 (written by a fourth grader) illustrates how students can include details.

Notice the name of the horse, the description of the tracks, the description of the watch, the explanation of the parents' absence. This student has written a detailed piece that allows the reader to "see" his story. The details make the piece interesting to a reader.

Structure

Definition

The term *structure* refers to the organization of a piece of writing: how the sentences/paragraphs/chapters communicate meaning by their order. Writing offers many different structures: none of them inherently "better" than others. Chronological order, order of importance, comparison and contrast, haiku, and newspaper editorial are all examples of common structures. At the elementary-school level, writers begin to learn that organization is important to help readers understand their content. As they work, these young writers begin to learn to use some of the more common structures found in writing. These structures make writing easier for them: story maps, Venn diagrams, and poetry patterns help them focus what they want to say.

Grade-level Applications and Examples

In grades K–3 structure concerns focus primarily on sequence of ideas (beginning, middle, end). Personal experience narratives, imaginative stories, reports based on personal observation as well as letters and poems are common organizational structures for writing at this level. The personal narrative piece written by John in Miss Wells' class (Chapter 2, Figure 2.2) illustrates the personal experience narrative structure: it is the story of the writer's first horse ride.

FIGURE 3.5. Details

Crystal Quartz Cave

One day, I needed a little space to just sit around, relax, and get away from it all, so I went outside and jumped on my horse named Scarlett. I explored the hills, the road, and so on. I came upon some snow, and in the snow I followed some small Jack Rabbit tracks to a deep cave completely made of Quartz Crystal. It was the most beautiful thing I ever saw in my entire life. It wasn't made by nature, it was man made. When I said "Hello" to see if anyone was there, my voice echoed through the cave. I looked at my gold trimmed, white watch it was seven thirty. I jumped on Scarlett and rode home. Mom & dad weren't home. I hoped they did not go out looking for me. Well, Mom & dad got home after 3 hours. They said they had gone for dinner and a play.

This student sequenced the ideas appropriately. The writing begins with the trip to the ranch, the first thing that happened in chronological order. The next two sentences discuss learning to ride, something that happened after arrival. The next paragraph tells about a particular trip the writer went on after learning to ride. The last sentence sums up the whole experience by telling which horse the writer favored among all those he rode on this trip.

In grades 4–6 students are ready to work with paragraph structure. They can begin to write paragraphs that state main ideas as a topic sentence, and they can organize paragraphs according to specialized structures such as cause and effect, comparison and contrast, time order, and so forth. Students at this level are ready to write expository papers (description, directions, explanation, cause and effect, comparison and contrast, summary, etc.) along with the personal-writing structures they began in earlier grades.

The piece of writing turned in to Mr. Thayer (Chapter 2, Figure 2.3) by Karl illustrates a specialized kind of explanation structure—the TV news report.

The writer has "explained" the central event in Shel Silverstein's poem "Jimmy Jet and the TV Set" as if it were a news item, following the demands of that structure. Notice the station and personnel identifications in the first sentence. Further, notice how the writer speaks directly to the audience, complete with a conclusion for the children ("So children, unless you want to . . ."). Notice as well how the piece concludes in the expected way ("That's all the news . . ."). This student has demonstrated a good understanding of this particular structure.

Mechanics

Definition

Mechanics is the term I prefer for grammatical correctness in writing. Other terms often used are "surface structure," "usage," and "editing concerns." Mechanics can refer to simple accuracy (Are the periods placed properly?) or it can refer to sophistication of grammatical stylistic choices (Does the writer use compound-complex sentences?). Mechanics are important, for done clumsily they can confuse a reader and even change intended meaning. Sometimes, however, mechanics are overemphasized, literally sweeping away a writer's competence in context, content, and structure. Because research has shown that grammar rules taught in isolation do not carry over to writing fluency, most teachers of writing address mechanical errors at the cleanup stage of writing after context, content, and structure have been controlled. Grammar minilessons focus on specific rules writers need to follow.

Modern reading theory tells us something important about mechanical errors. Frank Smith (1971) and researchers that followed him describe proficient reading as print sampling that uses only the amount of text required for comprehension rather than as detailed letter-by-letter processing. Editing, which depends on careful examination of each letter, each period, and each comma, is clearly a separate skill from reading. Particularly in reading where there is a high degree of background knowledge (such as when the reader is also the writer), proofreading is an extremely difficult task, especially for young students, who may not even see their errors. Correctness, then, often becomes a community responsibility: Gina, who is good at capitalization rules, chooses to help Joey and Esther by looking for capitalization errors in their writing. Joey, the best speller in their pod, helps Gina and Esther by looking for spelling errors in their writing. Esther, who never writes incomplete sentences, chooses to help Gina and Joey by looking for the correct placement of periods (and so on). Because the students have chosen their editing tasks based on their own skills, they begin to take ownership of the accuracy of their own and other students' writing.

Grade-level Applications and Examples

In grades K–3 appropriate mechanical concerns include completion of thoughts as sentences, use of transitions and conjunctions to connect ideas, conventional word endings, personal pronouns, contractions, singular possessives, verb tenses, subject-verb agreement, conventional spelling, punctuation, and capitalization.

It is important to note here, that out of this list, punctuation, spelling, and capitalization relate only to writing and need to be taught to every child. The rest of the list springs from spoken usage: particular children, especially students whose first language is not English, will need to work on particular items, but all students will not need instruction in all the items on the list. As teachers, we may choose to guide our students' spoken usage toward standard English or we may choose not to. As teachers of writing we need to make a clear distinction between spoken and written language, guiding our students toward standard written usage. (Register, or the context of the communication, is of course an important consideration, but that discussion is beyond the scope of this book.)

"My First Horse Ride" (Chapter 2, Figure 2.2) illustrates the proper use of the period by a young writer. Each sentence is a complete thought.

In grades 4–6, the list of mechanical concerns remains the same with several additions: sentence variety (simple, compound, and complex), use of homophones, and use of comparisons.

The essay about friends (the fourth-grade example of "context" above) illustrates the improper use of homophones: "your" is spelled the same way twice, although the first time it means "you are" and the second time it is second-person possessive. Furthermore, this essay illustrates the incorrect usage of a compound sentence (the next to last sentence.)

FIGURE 3.6. Transitions

THE FIGHT

One day while my
cousin, friend and I were walking home
we saw a boxer at the store when my dog
Dinkey a male redheeler came running
toward the boxer.The boxer grabbed
Dinkey's hind leg we were screaming
when my friend Bob who lived across us
got his gun, and followed the boxer when
he shot the boxer.Later we took him
to the vet.

The piece in Figure 3.6, "The Fight," illustrates the problems that sometimes surface for students working in a second language. This piece was written by a sixth-grader whose first language is Navajo. Notice the confusion between "when" and "then." This piece illustrates the improper "use of transitions" that would need to be taught to a few students, rather than to the entire class.

Process

Definition

A fifth component of writing is the process used by the writer to produce the product. While the sophistication of the activities writers carry out at each point in the process varies as students get older and more experienced, the components of the process remain the same.

Prewriting happens before a rough draft ever occurs. It includes brainstorming, discussions, drawing, dramatization, listening, reading, observing, selecting a topic, and identifying the context of the writing. Most theorists agree that well over 50 percent of writing time is devoted to some form of prewriting.

Drafting begins when pencil hits paper and sentences begin to be composed. It includes freewriting, reading what has been written, and deciding what to do next.

Revising occurs when a writer rereads a draft for ideas. Content and structure concerns are addressed in the revising stage, most often with the help of peer readers.

Editing focuses on sentence structure, word choice, and usage and mechanics. Most often it includes both attempts at self-editing and the help of an outside editor. Once editing is complete, the student generally rewrites and proofreads the final draft for mistakes in copying.

Publishing results in sharing the final draft. Teachers provide many different ways to publish student work: by displaying it on a bulletin board, by binding it into a class book, by printing it in a newsletter, by entering it in a contest, by sending it home to parents, by giving it as a gift, by sharing it in ad hoc groups, by reading it to the whole class from an author's chair, and so forth.

Applications and Examples

The following checklist (Bratcher and Larson, 1992) illustrates the writing process as one teacher used it for an instructional sequence in writing a personal narrative:

cluster map
partner checklist for topic, audience, and purpose
rough draft
revising worksheet
editing workshop
final copy submitted for class book

Students stapled the list on the front of their writing folders and then checked off each item as they completed it.

Figures 3.7 through 3.12 illustrate the above process as used by one fourth-grader. The cluster (Figure 3.7) shows how this student planned for writing about her trip to Havasupai Canyon (a tributary of the Grand Canyon). Notice that the cluster includes information on setting, time, and characters involved in the trip.

Figure 3.8, "partner checklist," illustrates how another student helped this writer add more details to her personal narrative.

The rough draft (Figure 3.9) and revising worksheet (Figure 3.10) illustrate how this student's partner made suggestions for a final draft. Notice the suggestions for more details.

The editing workshop sheet in Figure 3.11 illustrates how this pod of students divided up the mechanical checking for each other.

The final copy (Figure 3.12) illustrates the quality of work that was accepted for the class book. (The student's mother typed the personal narrative.) The final class book was bound and placed in the school library for other students to read.

FIGURE 3.7. Cluster

Cluster Map

FIGURE 3.8. Partner Checklist

PARTNER CHECKLIST

My partner is __Jane_____

His/Her topic is __Havasupi_____

This topic is about himself/herself (yes or no) __yes_____
It is interesting to the class (yes or no) __yes__
He/she wants to write about it (yes or no) __yes__

The purpose is ~~is~~ __Fun_____

The cluster contains (check off if it is there; circle if it is missing)
      place __✓_____
      (time)
      people __✓_____
      interesting details __✓_____

The cluster has the items numbered in order for telling the story __Yes__

__Veronica_____
SIGNATURE

FIGURE 3.9. Rough Draft

Going to HavaSupi

When I was 9 years old I went to Havasupi. I went with my friend, Katie, my dad, my dad's friend, my dad's friends son Eric, and Eric's friend Rubbin. We all went down to the South Rim of the Grand Canyon ~~and~~ and ate lunch. After lunch we got our back packs and went down the trail, On the trail, at ~~the~~ first it was switch backs for about a mile. Then it was straight. We had our own groups. Eric and Rubbin who stayed ahead. Katie and I who stayed in the middle. My Dad and his friend who stayed behind.

FIGURE 3.10. Revising Worksheet

REVISING WORKSHEET

1. My partner is JAne

2. His/Her topic is Going to Havasupi

3. His/Her personal narrative uses "I" to tell the story.   (yes or no)
yes

4. It is interesting to the class because ~~春玄~~ It is About
friends

5. I can tell he/she wanted to write about it because She had ~~pictures~~
pictures for it.

6. The purpose of this personal narrative is An adventure
(happy, sad, an adventure, a surprise, funny, or something else)

7. In the personal narrative.
    (a)   the setting is HavaSupi   .
    It is fine like it is ✓   or It needs more detail _____

    (b)   the time is Summer   .
    It is fine like it is ✓   or It needs more detail _____

    (c)   the characters are Katie, HerDad, Afriend, Eric, and Rubbin
    They are fine like they are ✓   or They need more detail _____

8. The thing I like the best about my partner's personal narrative is
All the adventures in it

9. One thing I'd like to know more about in this personal narrative is
What her horse's name was.
Veronica
SIGNATURE

FIGURE 3.11. Editing Workshop

EDITING WORKSHOP

Your pod is going to help each other clear up grammar and spelling mistakes in your personal narratives. In this workshop there will be four jobs: checking for complete sentences
checking for good use of capital letters
checking for spelling
checking for punctuation.

Each person in the pod will have one job. He/She will then look for that error in everyone's paper (including his/her own), so each pod member will have four papers to look for one thing in. There are three steps to this workshop.

1. Please choose jobs and then list which person has which job below:

checking for complete sentences Veronica

checking for good use of capital letters Paul and Felix

checking for spelling Jane

checking for punctuation Paul and Felix

2. If you find what you think is a mistake, circle it. The writer can then check to make sure what he/she has written is correct.

3. When you finish checking a paper, at the bottom of the last page write your job and initials to indicate that you are finished. (It might look like this--capitals/ SJB.)

FIGURE 3.12. Final Draft

GOING TO HAVASUPI

When I was nine years old I went to Havasupi. My dad said that I could invite one friend, so I invited my best friend Katie. My Dad invited Tom, his best friend. Tom has one son. His name is Aaron and Aaron came. Aaron got to invite a friend. He invited his best friend Rubbin.

We all went down to the South Rim of the Grand Canyon and ate lunch. After lunch we got our backpacks on and went down the trail. At first the trail was switchbacks for about a mile. Then it was straight. We all stayed in groups: Eric and Rubbin who stayed in front, Katie and I who stayed in the middle, and Tom and Dad, who stayed behind. As I said, we had our own groups, but once we all go together to eat lunch.

Katie and I stopped twice. Once we saw a sign that said four more miles. After a while Katie and I heard some running water, but we could not find what was making the sound until... SPLASH! We both fell into a creek. The reason why we fell was because we could not see the stream. It was covered by bright green bushes. After we fell we decided to soak our feet. While we were soaking our feet, we saw a little village. We were glad to see Havasupi was we were tired of walking; we did walk nine miles!

When we got to the motel and went into the lounge, we saw Aaron and Rubbin. I guess they planned to say, "Where were you guys?" because at the same time they said, "Where were you guys?"

Together Katie and I said, "Walking."

Then I had an idea to say "Where were you guys?" to Tom and Dad. I told Katie, Aaron, and Rubbin my plan. They all agreed, so when Tom and Dad got to the lounge Katie, Aaron, Rubbin, and I all said, "Where were you guys?"

Tom and Dad said, "Walking and looking at rocks."

We all went to the hotel room and got our bathing suits on. We went to a little river up a ways from the hotel. While Tom, Dad, Aaron, and Rubbin swam, Katie and I looked at rocks. We stayed there for about 30 minutes.

When we got back to the room, Aaron and Rubbin took a shower. That's when Katie and I discovered the light switch to the bathroom

FIGURE 3.12. Final Draft (continued)

was in the other room. So Katie and I just happily turned off the light. But when Tom and Dad heard the boys falling and yelling, they turned the light back on. The only problem with turning off the light was when we were taking our shower, off went the light!

In Havasupi there is only one place to eat, and it closes at 6 o'clock p.m., so after Aaron, Rubbin, Katie, and I had taken half of our shower in the dark, we went to eat. After we ate, we went back to the hotel room. We all did our own thing. Tom and Dad looked at the stars, Aaron and Rubbin played Nintendo, and Katie and I talked.

In the morning we walked to Havasu Falls, which is two miles away from the hotel. When we got to Havasu Falls, my dad told us about a rope swing. At Havasu Falls there are circles of rock, and in those circles of rock is water. I call them pools. Down away from the pools is a place to river raft. Aaron and Rubbin played on the rope swing, Katie and I played in the pools, and Tom and Dad went river rafting. Havasu Falls is 75 feet tall.

After about two hours, we started toward Mooney Falls. When we got to Mooney, we went down a trail and through two tunnels and we got to a chain that hangs down about 30 feet. By the time we got to the bottom of the chain, we were soaked from the sprays of Mooney. When we got down we had to hide behind a rock so we didn't get wetter. We stayed down there for about 15 minutes. Then we went back to the top. Mooney Falls is 200 feet tall.

On the way back from Mooney, Katie and I, Tom and Dad stopped at a mine. The boys were too far ahead, so they didn't get to come. Katie and I filled our pockets with pretty rocks. That night, Aaron and Rubbin, Katie and I, all took our showers in the dark.

That morning Tom, Aaron, and Rubbin left on foot. Later Dad, Katie, and I left on horses. Katie's horse was Shadow. My dad's was named Cinnamon. My horse's name was Taffy. The hike down is nine hours, but with horses it is only seven. I think it was more fun to ride up on horses than walk, but I'm not sure because since I couldn't reach the stirrups, it was a bouncy ride. The funny part about riding up was that Katie and I had horses because we were light, but my dad had a mule because he was heavier.

When we got back to the top, we met Aaron, Rubbin, and Tom. We all drove home. One thing for sure was Katie and I were glad to get those rocks out of our backpacks!

Chapter Summary

Healing teacher/grader schizophrenia depends on setting teaching objectives for writing assignments and then grading according to those objectives. To set objectives, we must examine the various pieces of the writing puzzle: context, content, structure, mechanics, and process. We must determine the grade-appropriate writing behaviors in each of these areas so that we may design instruction (and grades) accordingly.

EXERCISES

1. Find a copy of your state's guidelines for writing or your district's curriculum guide. For the grade you teach, classify the writing expectations according to the categories provided in this chapter.

2. Analyze your own writing according to the categories provided in this chapter. What areas are you strong in? What areas are you weaker in? Might these strengths and weaknesses affect how you teach writing?

3. Choose a paper from those in the appendix and analyze it according to the categories provided in this chapter.

References   Bratcher, Suzanne and Jan Larson. "Writing with fourth-graders: a personal narrative experience." Unpublished study. Flagstaff, AZ: DeMiguel Elementary School, 1992.

Language Arts Essential Skills, (Arizona Department of Education, February 1989, C. Diane Bishop, Superintendent); "Essential Skills," pp. 1–5.

Smith, Frank. *Understanding Reading.* New York: Holt, Rinehart, and Winston, 1971.

PART II

Evaluation Options

If we accept the premises that evaluation is communication and that instructional contexts and purposes differ, it follows that we need a repertoire of different evaluation strategies to match different teaching situations. This part classifies twenty grading techniques into four large categories and provides step-by-step instructions for using these techniques. Samples of student papers illustrate the grading techniques.

The four categories I have used here to classify the techniques are important to any discussion of evaluation. Sometimes I have heard teachers talk about management systems as if they were grading approaches, suggesting that portfolios were an alternative to criterion-referenced grading, for example. But a portfolio is a management system: it falls in a separate category from criterion-referenced grading. There are lots of different types of portfolios—analytic as well as holistic. So it is entirely possible to create a criterion-referenced portfolio!

The categories, then, are critical to an understanding of how grading works. Grading approaches, response strategies, management systems, and evaluation styles work together—they are not isolated techniques. (Any grading system will contain all the categories.) By "grading approaches" I mean options teachers have for determining letter or number grades. By "response strategies" I mean options teachers have for communicating the grades they have determined to their students. By "management systems" I mean options for determining longer-term grades (grades for a nine-week session or for a year). By "evaluation styles" I mean power options—will the decision making lie in the hands of the teacher, the students, or both? By "hybrids" I mean the various configurations of the combinations and mixtures of these categories. (The criterion-referenced portfolio mentioned above is an example of a hybrid.)

CHAPTER 4

Approaches to Grading

Like almost any behavior we might name, grading approaches can be conceptualized as occurring along several different continua. The continuum I find most helpful for thinking about grading approaches looks like the one below, with holistic grading at one end of the spectrum and analytic grading at the other end:

Holistic measures   Analytic scales

In this chapter I discuss six options within "grading approaches." They are present on the holistic—analytic continuum below:

Holistic Approaches

Anchor   Cluster   Questions   Primary   Assignment   Criterion
                                                    trait   generated   referenced

I have used all of these approaches in my own teaching, and I have seen them all used by other teachers. All of them can be useful (just as all of them can be useless), depending on the particular writing assignment and its instructional purpose. I begin the explanations with analytic approaches simply because they are easier to explain, not because they are somehow superior to holistic approaches. The order of presentation, then, is arbitrary—no hierarchy is intended.

Analytic Approaches

Analytic approaches attempt to break a piece of writing into its component parts. Analytic strategies of grading are based on the assumption that the quality of a piece of writing is the sum of the quality of each component of the writing. Sometimes the characteristics of good writing that form the parts to be evaluated are identified by the individual grader and sometimes by an outside agency (like the writers of curriculum guides or specialists in a state department of education). Once the parts have been identified and described, individual student writing is compared against a scale that has been created from the chosen characteristics. Some teachers do this identification in their heads; others make use of written rubrics (grading guides). The biggest advantage of rubrics is that they communicate the teacher's grading guidelines to the student. Rubrics often avoid the common complaint that a grade was "subjective" (usually meaning unfair). They also communicate a clear message to the writer about what the evaluator thinks is successful and what he or she thinks needs more work.

Two analytic options appear on the extreme end of the continuum: criterion-referenced evaluation and assignment-generated evaluation. We next turn to these options.

Criterion-referenced Evaluation

The most atomistic analytic approach is criterion-referenced evaluation, which attempts to take into account every possible criterion of good writing at any level. A criterion-referenced evaluation system would look at Chapter 3 of this book (or a similar source) and make a list of all the items in context, content, structure, mechanics, and process that are appropriate to the grade-level being taught. Items in the list would then be weighted by points, and a grade could be determined. For example, a criterion-referenced scoring sheet for a fourth-grade expository writing (based on the Arizona Essential Skills document in Chapter 3) might look like Figure 4.1. Henry, a fourth-grade student in Mrs. Spiro's class, has turned in the essay in Figure 4.2. Mrs. Spiro grades Henry's essay using the criterion-referenced scoring sheet. Her completed scoring sheet looks like Figure 4.3.

Some Advantages of Criterion-referenced Evaluation
a. It evaluates each of the identified skills of the good writer.
b. It lists for the student everything the evaluator wants him or her to work on.

Some Disadvantages of Criterion-referenced Evaluation
a. It assumes that the quality of a piece of writing is the sum of its parts.
b. It evaluates a product without reference to current instruction.
c. It can overwhelm both students and teachers.

FIGURE 4.1. Criterion-referenced Grading Sheet

TOTAL POINTS POSSIBLE: 100   TOTAL POINTS EARNED: _____

CONTEXT (20 pts.)   Points Earned: _____
   purpose of the writing identified
   reader identified
   writer's stance identified

CONTENT (20 pts.)   Points Earned: _____
   topic is narrowed
   ideas are complete
   main idea is clear
   details are tailored to the main idea

STRUCTURE (20 pts.)   Points Earned: _____
   sequence of ideas (beginning, middle, end)
   follows assigned structure (expository form)
   paragraphs contain topic sentences

MECHANICS (20 pts.)   Points Earned: _____
   completion of thoughts as sentences
   use of transitions and conjunctions to connect ideas
   conventional word endings
   personal pronouns
   contractions
   singular possessives
   verb tenses
   subject-verb agreement
   conventional spelling
   punctuation
   capitalization
   sentence variety (simple, compound, and complex)
   use of homophones
   use of comparisons

PROCESS (20 pts.)   Points Earned: _____
   prewriting turned in
   partner checklist for topic, audience, and purpose
   rough draft
   revising worksheet
   editing workshop
   final copy submitted for class book

FIGURE 4.2. Henry's Essay

By Henry

The San Francisco Peaks

The San Francisco Peaks

are north of Flagstaff, AZ. They

erupted about 1.8 million years

ago and built up over a long

period to form what they are

now. They're about 12,600

feet high and are made up of

five main peaks.

The San Francisco Peaks

have an interresting history. The Peaks

erupted from 1.8 million years ago

to 400,000 years ago. The Peaks

where named by a group called the

FIGURE 4.2. Henry's Essay (continued)

Franciscans. When the Franciscans
went to convert the Hopi, they gave
the Peaks their name.

The Peaks have many kinds of
trees on them. Going up the Peaks is
like going north to the artic circle.
It gets colder and less humid. This
is the order the tree grow up the
Peaks: Juniper-Pinyon woodland,
Ponderosa Pine forest, Mixed
conifer and Spruce-Fir forest.

There are also plants and
animals on the Peaks. There are

FIGURE 4.2. Henry's Essay (continued)

animals like dwarf shrews, lincoln
sparrows, hawks, hummingbirds,
chickadees, steel jays, marrianelk
and mule deer living on the Peaks.
There are 80 kinds of plants on
the Peaks like lupine, wild strawberrys,
wild tuft, groundse l and buttercups.

Bibliography
Pewe, T. L, and Updike, R. G, San
Francisco Peaks, A Guide to
the geogly Flagstaff, Arizona,
Northern Azizona Society
of Science and Art, Inc, 1976

Aitchison, S. W, and Breed W. J,
San Francisco Peaks Flagstaff,
Arizona, Museum of
Northern Arizona, 1989

FIGURE 4.3. Criterion-referenced Grading Sheet for "San Francisco Peaks"

TOTAL POINTS POSSIBLE: 100   TOTAL POINTS EARNED: ___74___

CONTEXT (20 pts.) *about 7 points per category*   Earned: ___6___
    purpose *partially—the last paragraph omits animal and plant life*
    reader identified *no*
    writer's stance identified *no*

CONTENT (20 pts.) *5 points per category*   Earned: ___20___
    topic is narrowed *yes—the San Francisco Peaks*
    ideas are complete *yes*
    main idea is clear *yes*
    details are tailored to the main idea *yes*

STRUCTURE (20 pts.) *about 7 points per category*   Earned: ___18___
    sequence of ideas *yes—past to present*
    follows assigned structure (expository form) *yes*
    paragraphs contain topic sentences *partially—paragraph 3 wanders from trees to climate
        and back to trees again; trees should be part paragraph 4—plants and animals*

MECHANICS (20 pts.) *1.5 points per category*   Earned: ___16___
    completion of thoughts as sentences *yes*
    use of transitions and conjunctions to connect ideas *yes*
    conventional word endings *yes*
    personal pronouns *none needed*
    contractions *yes—paragraph 1*
    singular possessives *none needed*
    verb tenses *yes—past and present*
    subject-verb agreement *yes*
    conventional spelling *six errors—paragraph 2 "interresting", "where" for "were"; paragraph 3
      "artic"; paragraph 4 "duarf", "strawberrys"*
    punctuation *yes*
    capitalization *two errors—"lincoln" and "marrian"*
    sentence variety *partial—one complex sentence in paragraph 2 "When the Franciscans"—
      the rest are simple*
    use of homophones *yes*
    use of comparisons *yes*

PROCESS (20 pts.) *about 3 points per category*   Earned: ___14___
    process evidence not supplied here: turned in
    prewriting turned in *yes*
    partner checklist for topic, audience, and purpose *no*
    rough draft *yes*
    revising worksheet *yes*
    editing workshop *no*
    final copy submitted for class book *yes*

Assignment-generated Evaluation

A second type of analytic evaluation is based on criteria generated by a particular assignment. In this approach, someone—the teacher, the students, or everyone together—generates a grading guide based on the particular assignment. Sometimes these rubrics look like criterion-referenced grading sheets tailored for a particular type of writing (expository or personal narrative, for example); most, however, have fewer criteria—six to ten. An example of an assignment-generated rubric for primary students (grades 1–3) writing friendly letters to a character from a reading assignment might look like this:

Letter is to someone in the story we read (+, −)
Letter mentions something from the story (+, ✓, −)
Letter tells something about the writer (+, ✓, −)
Letter form is followed (+, ✓, −)
    date
    Dear _____,
    paragraphs are indented properly
    Love or Your friend,
    signature
Periods are in the right places (+, ✓, −)
Pod partners have made suggestions (+, ✓, −)
Final copy is neat and ready to mail (+, ✓, −)
Grade (+, ✓, −)

Miriam turns in the letter illustrated in Figure 4.4.

We can evaluate Miriam's letter using the rubric. The letter is addressed to Koko, the main character in the story. It mentions that Miriam is glad Koko got a new cat and tells several things about her pets. The letter form is good (the date, opening and closing, her signature—the P.S. is something she added her-self!), but the paragraphs are not indented properly. The periods are correct, Miriam has participated in her pod-revision group, and the final copy is neat. Mr. Avery, her teacher, gives Miriam a "+" on her letter, but suggests that she make one more copy, correcting her paragraphing before she mails it.

Some Advantages of Assignment-generated Evaluation
a. It communicates to students the goals of the particular assignment.
b. It changes as instruction changes.

Some Disadvantages of Assignment-generated Evaluation
a. It may not be sensitive to a particular strength or weakness in an individual student's writing.
b. It may emphasize the differences in writing tasks rather than the similarities.

FIGURE 4.4. Miriam's Letter

March 10

Dear Koko,

I am Miriam. I am glad you got a new cat. I am getting a new cat today. He is going to be black and white. I am going to be so glad. I love animals especially gorillas. I love you. Last year my dog got ran over and I cried too, but I got another dog. I got a hamster and he is gray and white. His name is Sqeekers.

your Friend,
Miriam

P.S. write back soon.

Holistic Approaches

Holistic approaches to measuring writing quality evaluate the success (or lack of it) of a whole piece of writing. Evaluation, by its very nature, compares a piece of writing to something outside itself; holistic grading depends on comparisons with other pieces of writing rather than on comparisons against a predetermined scale of criteria. Two different types of holistic measures are discussed here: "anchor" grading (sometimes called "benchmark," "prototype," or "touchstone") and "cluster" grading (within-group comparison grading). "Impressionistic" grading, a sort of pseudo-holistic grading, which is often referred to as "holistic grading," causing confusion, is also discussed.

Anchor Evaluation

In this approach, sample papers *from outside the classroom* provide the guidelines for grades. The term "anchor" implies its purpose: to keep individual grades from "drifting" from a common standard agreed upon by evaluators. Anchors are drawn from a large sample of student writing that responded to the same assignment. The student writers of these pieces wrote them under similar conditions, but the samples are not actually chosen from one classroom.

For example, the third grade teachers in one school might collect poems from their students for one year. At the end of that year they would pool all of their student work. As a team, they would choose one or two poems (anchors) that were representative of "+" writing—high "+" and low "+", one or two poems that were representative of "✓" writing, and one or two poems that were representative of "−" writing. The following year each teacher would refer to the anchors from the year before in grading poems from third graders in his or her classroom. Current student poems would be evaluated by their similarity to the anchors. If a poem were more like the "+" anchor than like the "✓" anchor, it would receive a grade of "+." But if it were more like the "✓," it would receive a "✓." Poems that could not be classified easily would be referred to two more teachers to grade. When two out of the three teachers agreed on the category, that grade would be assigned. Of course, the same procedure could be used to set anchors for expository writing, personal narratives, or any genre.

The poems in Figures 4.5 through 4.9 illustrate anchor evaluation. They are examples of anchors for poems about toys by third-graders. (These anchors were chosen by teachers in the state of Arizona and are part of the Arizona Student Assessment Program, a performance-based writing test published by the Riverside Publishing Company.) The explanations that follow each anchor explain the rationale for its being representative of the particular point score it illustrates. Once evaluators are familiar with the anchors, they then are able to categorize other poems by their likeness to particular anchors.

FIGURE 4.5. Anchor 1

WRITING

EXERCISE F: 40 minutes

Check List

- ☑ I checked my poem to make sure I wrote about how my toy looks, sounds, and feels.
- ☑ I checked my poem to make sure I wrote about how I feel about my toy.
- ☑ I looked at my poem to make sure it is written in lines instead of paragraphs.
- ☑ I counted to make sure I wrote at least 6 lines.
- ☐ I decided how to arrange the lines in a pattern.
- ☐ I checked all the words I wrote for spelling errors.

Final Draft

TITLE: My truch is rogh.

Because it was made
rogh. I like my truck
because it is in importtom
The hude feels like it is
smooth.
My truck say crazy monter.

SCORE POINT: 1   Though this paper does center around the toy, its
lack of pattern of organization and its sparseness and lack of
completeness keep it at the "1" level.

FIGURE 4.6. Anchor 1 (second example)

WRITING

EXERCISE F: 40 minutes

Check List

- ☒ I checked my poem to make sure I wrote about how my toy looks, sounds, and feels.
- ☒ I checked my poem to make sure I wrote about how I feel about my toy.
- ☒ I looked at my poem to make sure it is written in lines instead of paragraphs.
- ☒ I counted to make sure I wrote at least 6 lines.
- ☒ I decided how to arrange the lines in a pattern.
- ☒ I checked all the words I wrote for spelling errors.

SCORE POINT:1   This is not a poem describing a toy, but a
narrative about the adventures of "Sir Hiss;" clearly the writer
has misunderstood the requirements of the assigned task.

TITLE: Sir had to walk 3,560 milse
Sir Hiss, Missed The train,
He was slithering to slow   so he had
to Slither to New York, He lived in
Washington It was 3,560 miles, but
he was tired on the 500th, mile
So, He had to stop in hotsprings
North Dokta, He had 460 milesto
go, He started out in the
morning very early, He had
to, Jump offa cliff 300feet high
and he was there and he
met his freinds. THE END

FIGURE 4.7. Anchor 2

WRITING

EXERCISE F: 40 minutes

Check List

☑ I checked my poem to make sure I wrote about how my toy looks, sounds, and feels.

☑ I checked my poem to make sure I wrote about how I feel about my toy.

☑ I looked at my poem to make sure it is written in lines instead of paragraphs.

☑ I counted to make sure I wrote at least 6 lines.

☑ I decided how to arrange the lines in a pattern.

☑ I checked all the words I wrote for spelling errors.

Final Draft

TITLE: *My Car*

A car is yellow
It tastes like sour grapes.
It smells like a car.
It looks like a flash of lighting
It feels like metal
It makes me to drive it.

SCORE POINT: 2 This typical 2 is merely a list of sensory impressions, some inappropriate ("tastes like sour grapes") plus a reaction to the toy, per the checklist. It has no creativity and does nothing to enliven the object it describes.

FIGURE 4.8. Anchor 3

 WRITING

EXERCISE F: 40 minutes

Check List
☐ I checked my poem to make sure I wrote about how my toy looks, sounds, and feels.
☐ I checked my poem to make sure I wrote about how I feel about my toy.
☐ I looked at my poem to make sure it is written in lines instead of paragraphs.
☐ I counted to make sure I wrote at least 6 lines.
☐ I decided how to arrange the lines in a pattern.
☐ I checked all the words I wrote for spelling errors.

Final Draft

TITLE: _____MY bike_____

My Bike is red and black
I ride it quite alot
The seat on it is cushined
And Sometimes it is hot
And when I ride it I feel great
And when I ride someWare I'm never late

SCORE POINT: 3   Though short, this poem does describe the toy through various sense images, and the writer is able to successfully incorporate both rhyme and meter.   The creativity of this paper raises it above the 2/3 line.

FIGURE 4.9. Anchor 4

 WRITING

EXERCISE F: 40 minutes

Check List

☒ I checked my poem to make sure I wrote about how my toy looks, sounds, and feels.

☒ I checked my poem to make sure I wrote about how I feel about my toy.

☒ I looked at my poem to make sure it is written in lines instead of paragraphs.

☒ I counted to make sure I wrote at least 6 lines.

☒ I decided how to arrange the lines in a pattern.

☒ I checked all the words I wrote for spelling errors.

Final Draft

TITLE: *My Cat*

My cat looks pretty and she's got a laddybug.
On her pawse she loohs so cute every night,
I turn on my light and look at her.
I tuke care of her very much.
I let nobody to nuch her or drop her.
I leav it on my night stun by the light.
And it is importunt to me because my,
Mom guve it to me and I tuke care or it
very much and good.

SCORE POINT:4 Though this paper is not strong on physical description, the relationship between writer and toy is well described, as well as the setting in which the toy is kept. The emotional attachment between writer and toy is well established.

The poem in Figure 4.10 was written to the same assignment that the anchors were written to. This poem, "Fuzzy Bear," is more like the "4 point" anchor. The relationship between the writer and the toy is well described. The setting in which the toy is kept is also well described. The emotional attachment is well established. Furthermore, the poem contains physical description of the toy as well as some rhyme. "Fuzzy Bear," then, would be scored "4."

Some Advantages of Anchor Evaluation
a. More than one person is involved in determining what quality of writing constitutes a particular level of work or grade.
b. Once the evaluator is familiar with the anchors, this is probably the fastest way to determine a grade.

Some Disadvantages of Anchor Evaluation
a. It is isolated from instruction and does not allow for different emphases in grading over time.
b. It provides only a grade to a student. There is no systematic feedback provided on what the student has done well or what he or she needs to keep working on.

Cluster Grading

In this approach papers are compared not against outside examples, but against papers within the class group. Here's how it works. An entire set of papers from a single class on a single assignment is read more than once. (For cluster grading to work, the pieces of writing must have something in common. Most teachers who use cluster grading design assignments that have a common structure—say poetry or exposition or imaginative stories—but that allow for individual topic choice.) On the first reading, the evaluator makes three stacks of papers as he or she reads. One stack represents "good" papers. A second stack represents papers that clearly "need improvement." A third stack represents papers that are somewhere "in between." A second reading of the papers validates the first impression: some papers may be moved from one stack to another. At this point papers in the "good" stack may be assigned a grade of "+," papers in the "needs improvement" stack may be assigned a "−," and so on. If, however, a five-point scale ("1–5" or "+, ✓+, ✓, ✓−, −" or "A–F") is used, a third reading is required. At this point the three stacks become five. The "good" stack is divided into an "A" stack and a "B" stack. The "needs improvement stack" is divided into an "F" stack and a "D" stack. The "in between" stack is divided among the "B" stack, the "C" stack, and the "D" stack. A final rapid reading of each stack validates the evaluator's decisions.

Let's look at an example. Mr. Martinez teaches fourth grade. He has just finished teaching a poetry unit, and his students have handed in their poems

FIGURE 4.10. Sample Poem

WRITING

EXERCISE F: 40 minutes

Check List

☑ I checked my poem to make sure I wrote about how my toy looks, sounds, and feels.

☑ I checked my poem to make sure I wrote about how I feel about my toy.

☑ I looked at my poem to make sure it is written in lines instead of paragraphs.

☑ I counted to make sure I wrote at least 6 lines.

☑ I decided how to arrange the lines in a pattern.

☑ I checked all the words I wrote for spelling errors.

Final Draft

TITLE: Fuzzy Bear

Cute and cutley,
I And very soft!
I love her,
She is my own.
She is very furry,
But I still love her.
She stays on my bed,
And waits tell I get home.
She came from santa,
At the north pole
Smells like a baby,
Day and night,
Very soundless,
And she sleeps with me at night.

to be graded. On a quick first reading some of the poems stand out as carefully constructed—as "good" poems he can be enthusiastic about. He puts these poems in one stack. A few of the poems stand out as having been carelessly tossed together—as "weak" poems he is disappointed in. He puts them in a second stack. The rest of the poems are somewhere in between—they have characteristics that he is enthusiastic about as well as characteristics that disappoint him. He puts them in a third stack. Since he does not wish to make finer distinctions than "+," "✓," and "−," he simply rereads his stacks, validating his grouping. He switches a few poems here and there—Suzy's poem (one of the first he read) doesn't seem as strong as the rest of the poems in the "+" pile, so he moves it to the "✓" pile. Isaac's poem, on the other hand, seems stronger on a second reading than he first thought. He moves it from the "✓" pile to the "+" pile. Once this second reading is complete, he places the grades on the poems, according to stack. He then makes a rapid survey of each stack, making sure he still agrees with his grades.

Some Advantages of Cluster Grading
a. It compares writers to their immediate peers, to students who have had the same instruction as well as the same assignment.
b. Once the evaluator is familiar with this system, it is a relatively fast method.

Some Disadvantages of Cluster Grading
a. It provides only a grade to a student. There is no systematic feedback provided on what the student has done well or what he or she needs to keep working on.
b. It can create rivalry among student writers in a class.
c. It depends on the intuitional evaluation of a single grader.

Impressionistic Grading

Impressionistic grading is sometimes referred to as holistic grading, but it is really the "subjective" grading most of us objected to when we were students. All grading is subjective (that is, based on the evaluator's value system), but impressionistic grading has the added drawback that nowhere are the values made explicit, even by pointing to writing that illustrates the values being sought. Impressionistic grading is therefore less defensible and less useful as a method of communication. As a quick method of categorizing papers it is probably reliable—if the teacher has had lots of experience grading and if he or she does not have any clues as to the identity of the writer. But even if the teacher is relatively inexperienced, impressionistic evaluation can be a useful tool in the interim stages of writing. For example, when Anna comes to Ms. Lehmann's desk with a first draft and asks "How's my story?" she reads it through rapidly and answers on her impressions—"I really like the excitement when you found your puppy, but I want to know more about what he looks like."

Some Advantages of Impressionistic Grading
a. It is very fast.
b. Since it is traditional, it is often accepted by parents.

Some Disadvantages of Impressionistic Grading
a. It is personally based, subject to the enthusiasms and irritations of the moment.
b. It can be attacked as "subjective."

Analytic/Holistic Combinations

On the grading approach continuum, as on any continuum, there are approaches that cannot easily be classified with approaches on the two ends. Primary-trait evaluation and questions for grading both fall somewhere on the middle of the continuum. They have characteristics of holistic evaluation as well as characteristics of analytic evaluation.

Primary-trait Evaluation

Primary-trait evaluation is similar to criterion-referenced evaluation in that writing is evaluated against a list of criteria, but in this approach, the list is not intended to be exhaustive: it consists of only a few items, and the piece of writing is evaluated as a whole on this small list of criteria.

A primary-trait rubric designed to evaluate expository writing (directions for a game) by primary students might look something like this:

The piece is presented in direction format
The piece is focused on one game
The writing describes the game (the object of the game, what is needed to play, and how to win)

The teacher, Mrs. Garcia, uses a "+," "✓," "−" system to grade with. Floyd turns in the paper in Figure 4.11. Using the primary trait rubric, Mrs. Garcia gives Floyd's writing a "+": the paper is set up in a 1–5 list (like directions) and it tells the necessary information about Scrabble (that the object of the game is to make words from letters, that you need the Scrabble game and more than one player to play. and that you win by being the first player to run out of letters with none left to draw).

FIGURE 4.11. Floyd's Paper

This is how to play
Scrabble.
1. You make a word and
get so more letters then
you put them down and
let the other play
go.   2. you need to have
one, two, three or four
player's to play 3. you need
the game   and some
players. 4. and the first
player to run out of and
no words in the bag wins
5. if you don't play the game
right. you get kicked out of
the game.   Floyd

Natelle, another student in Mrs. Garcia's class, turns in the paper in Figure 4.12. Using the primary trait guide, Mrs. Garcia gives Natelle's paper a "—": the paper is not set up in direction format, rather it is written like an essay; the description of the game does not include the object of the game (a form of chase) or the fact that there is not really a winner and loser; the writing wanders off into other games (building a snowman, baseball, and bubblegum). Mrs. Garcia suggests that Natelle read some of her classmates' stories and then talks to her about her own. She suggests that Natelle do a revision to raise her grade.

Some Advantages of Primary-trait Evaluation
a. It focuses the student on a small number of instructional items.
b. It is highly responsive to instruction.

Some Disadvantages of Primary-trait Evaluation
a. It may allow students to de-emphasize past instruction.
b. It may overlook some important criteria.

Questions for Grading

Another approach to grading is based on a set of questions. Sometimes these questions may be preset, like the journalist's questions; sometimes they may be generated for the particular assignment. Questions have analytical characteristics because they focus the evaluator on a set of specific items; they have holistic characteristics because they take into account the whole of the piece for the answer to any particular question. An example of this approach, appropriate for intermediate students writing a story, might be the "W" questions. The evaluation guide might look something like this:

The story answers the following questions:
Who? (20%)
What? (20%)
When? (20%)
Where? (20%)
Why? (20%)

Kassandra, a student in Mr. Ruggles' class, turns in the story in Figure 4.13. Using the questions to guide his grading, Mr. Ruggles gives Kassandra's story 90%. Her story does a good job with "who" (full credit—20%). Chica is a clearly described, whimsical character. Her story also does a good job with "what" (full credit—20%). Chili peppers are described (how they grow, their hot characteristics, how they can be neutralized, that they are canned, etc.). The "when" of the story is there, but less clear (partial credit—15%). We know it happens at night, but that is all. We don't know (though we might guess) what time of year it is or how old the narrator is at the time of the story.

FIGURE 4.12. Natelle's Paper

Do you Know how to play
not it. I know how to
play not it it is fun.
This how you play not it
you have to put your
hand in the ather people
hand then Who ever the
last one to take out there
hand they are it. It is fun
game to play out side. We
Play lot of fun.game. We
fell so tired. We biut a
snowman out side can
you biut one. ~~Then~~ We

FIGURE 4.12. Natelle's Paper (continued)

know are rules. Do you
know your rules. Do you
know how to play baseball
we have lot of people.
Do you know how to play
bubble gum. We play like
this you have to put
all our hand in the
ather hand they you have
to say bubble gum
bubble gum.
                    Natelle

FIGURE 4.13. Kassandra's Story

CHICA: THE WALKING TALKING CHILI PEPPER

by Kassandra

I was asleep in bed when I heard a sound. I got up and shined my flashlight around the room. Then I went downstairs to see what was the matter. Still looking around with my flashlight, I opened the door and there it was: Chica, the walking, talking Chili Pepper!

Chica was bright red as many chili peppers tend to be. She wore a bright pink visor around her stem. Her earrings were orange hoops and her eyes were bright yellow. She came up to me and tried to touch me in greeting. I touched her back and accidentally - I'd like to think - she burned me a bit since she was a hot pepper! I asked her if she wanted to have a glass of milk but since milk neutralizes the stinging burn that a pepper can give. But she said the milk would make her less hot so when I suggested it she ran and hid.

I looked everywhere with my flashlight and just when I was ready to give up I found Chica in my cellar staring up at all the jars of pickled peppers I had canned She spoke enough English to ask me, pointing up toward the jars of peppers, "Chica's friends up there?" She stared at me and her face had a confused look upon it. She trembled in fear until I said, "No, they are not your friends so don't worry." She calmed down. Then said, "Chica very hungry. Prepare a nice feast for one hungry chili pepper girl. By the way, you boy or girl?" I told her I was a boy and then she asked if I spoke the language of the Chili Pepper. I told her no. She gazed up at me with her big yellow eyes.

During our awkward conversation in the kitchen Chica told me she had popped down off my chili plant in the garden then realized she could walk and talk.

Chica asked me if perhaps she could sleep in a pot with flowers in them. Then, she said, she'd feel at home. So I put her gently in a flowerpot of Colorado daisies. I read her a story, Hansel and Gretel. She got a bit scared from it but I told her I was not the witch.

After Chica had gone to sleep in the flowerpot, I laid down in my own bed when I heard a noise outside...who knows? Maybe...it could be Tom the walking talking Tomato!

Likewise, the "where" is a bit fuzzy (partial credit—15%). We know the story takes place in the kitchen, but it is not described. The why of the story is clear (full credit—20%). A noise has awakened the narrator. The ending of the story—another noise—suggests another story!

Here is an example of assignment-generated questions for grading. Mrs. Washington teaches second grade. Her students have just finished studying the body. She asks each student to choose an organ and write an acrostic poem about that organ. She creates these questions for grading:

Does your poem use all of the letters of the organ's name?
Does your poem tell at least three things about the organ?

Georgia, a student in Mrs. Washington's class, turns in poem in Figure 4.14. Using sun, cloud, and rain stickers for her "grades," Mrs. Washington puts a sun sticker on Georgia's poem because the answer to both questions is "yes": Georgia's poem uses all the letters in "liver," and it tells three things about the liver (that it cleans the blood, that people die without a liver, and that mammals other than humans have livers, too).

Andrew turns in the poem in Figure 4.15. Mrs. Washington puts a cloud sticker on Andrew's poem because the answer to one of the questions is a "yes" and the answer to the second question is "no": Andrew's poem uses all the letters in "kidney," but it only tells only one correct thing about kidneys (that they fight germs). Mrs. Washington asks Andrew to redo the kidney center and rewrite his poem.

Some Advantages of Questions for Grading
a. They can offer a new way of looking at writing.
b. They can be tailored to the particular assignment.

Some Disadvantages of Questions for Grading
a. They may be prejudicial to one aspect of a piece of writing, overlooking other important features.
b. If overused, they may be ignored by students.

Chapter Summary

Grading approaches can be classified along a continuum with analytic approaches at one end and holistic approaches at the other. Analytic approaches (criterion-referenced evaluation and assignment-generated evaluation) are based on the assumption that a piece of writing is equal to the sum of its parts. They, therefore, attempt to identify and list the parts of the writing being targeted for instruction. Student work is graded by reference to the list.

FIGURE 4.14. Georgia's Poem

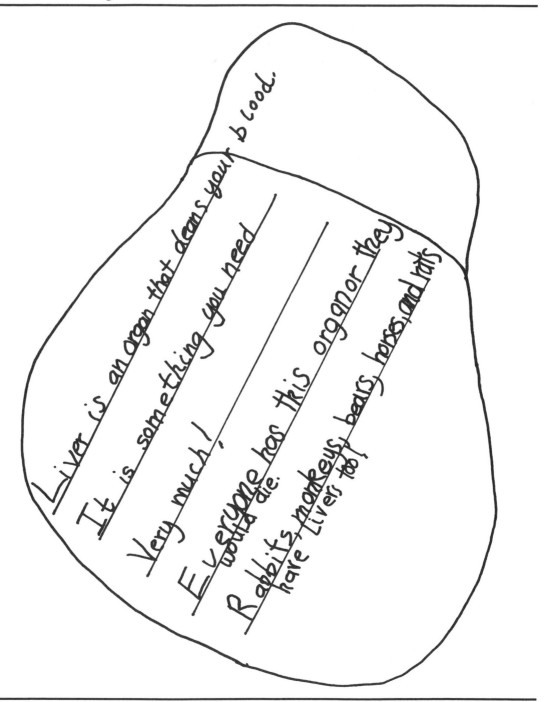

Liver is an organ that cleans your blood.
It is something you need
Very much!
Everyone has this organ or they
would die.
Rabbits monkeys, bears, horses, and rats
have livers too!

FIGURE 4.15. Andrew's Poem

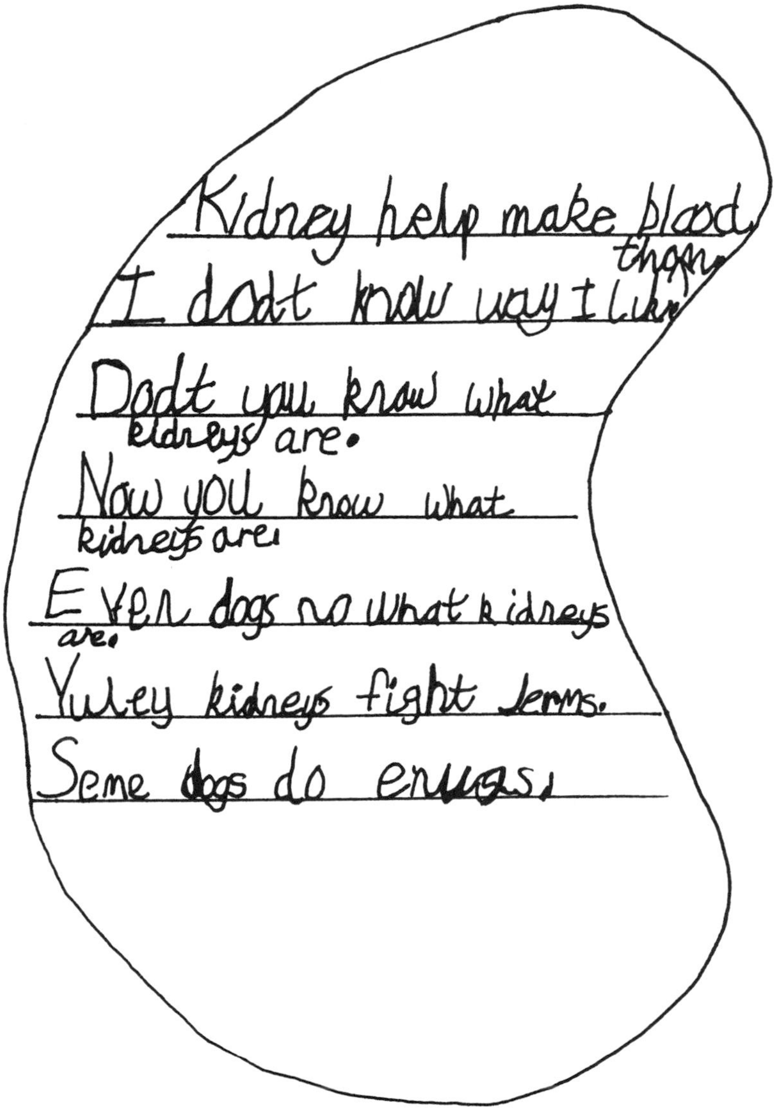

Kidney help make blood.
I dodt know way I like them.
Dodt you know what kidreys are.
Now you know what kidreys are.
Even dogs no what kidreys are.
Yuley kidneys fight germs.
Seme dogs do enuess.

Holistic approaches, on the other hand, look at a piece of writing as a whole. They ask the question "How does this piece of writing work?" They do not examine each puzzle piece separately. So, for example, mechanics are noticed unless they call attention to themselves—if there are so many errors that the piece is unintelligible or noticeably flawed. (The same is true for context, structure, and content.) There are two common holistic approaches: anchor evaluation and cluster grading.

Primary-trait scoring and questions for grading fall somewhere on the middle of the continuum, between analytic and holistic approaches. They examine a piece of writing as a whole, but they do so against a list of a small number of criteria.

EXERCISES

For Analytic Approaches

1. From a school curriculum guide or from your state's guidelines, make a criterion-referenced rubric for poetry written by intermediate writers (grades 4–6).

2. Using the same tools as in Exercise 1, make a criterion-referenced rubric for another kind of writing at a primary level.

3. Choose a piece of writing from the Appendix. First, design an assignment that the writing might be responding to. Next, using your school or state guidelines (or the guidelines provided in Chapter 3), design an assignment-generated rubric. Grade the paper accordingly.

For Holistic Approaches

4. Using the anchors reproduced in the text, score the poem in Figure 4.16.

5. As a group, locate one complete set of papers from a classroom. Take turns grading the set using a "+," "✓," "−" system of cluster grading. Compare the final grades. On how many papers did you agree? Discuss the papers you disagreed on.

6. Using the same set of papers in Exercise 5, as a group choose an anchor for the "+," "✓," "−" groups. (This exercise is only a simulation, anchors would never be chosen from one set of papers!)

For Holistic/Analytic Combinations

7. From the criterion-referenced rubric you created in Exercise 2, make a primary-trait rubric to use early in the year and a second one to use late in the year.

FIGURE 4.16. Poem to Score

WRITING

EXERCISE F: 40 minutes

Check List

☑ I checked my poem to make sure I wrote about how my toy looks, sounds, and feels.

☑ I checked my poem to make sure I wrote about how I feel about my toy.

☑ I looked at my poem to make sure it is written in lines instead of paragraphs.

☑ I counted to make sure I wrote at least 6 lines.

☑ I decided how to arrange the lines in a pattern.

☑ I checked all the words I wrote for spelling errors.

Final Draft

TITLE: *the cookie monter*

One day there was the cookie monter
he was runing because therwas
A big runing fast the the cookie
monter run fast he can but
the men get the
cookie monter

8. Find a paper in the Appendix that is appropriate to the rubrics you created in Exercise 7. Using your rubrics, grade it twice. How do the grades compare?

9. Choose a second paper from the Appendix. Design (or choose) a set of questions for grading that are appropriate to the topic. Evaluate the paper using your questions. Trade papers with someone else in your group. Using his or her questions, grade his or her paper. Have him or her grade yours. Compare your grades.

CHAPTER 5

Response Strategies

Response strategies are techniques that teachers use to communicate the grades they have arrived at by using one of the approaches in Chapter 4. There is no hard-and-fast pairing of particular response strategies with particular grading approaches: a student conference may be centered around a primary-trait assessment of the piece of writing, an assignment-generated rubric, or a holistic anchor paper, for example. Three common ways of responding to student writing are with oral responses, with written responses, and with grades without comments. While these ways of responding are very different in how they communicate, all of them can be useful at one time or another.

Oral Responses

Writing Conferences

Using this response method, teachers sit down with students one-on-one and orally discuss the evaluation. Usually a rubric, an anchor paper from outside the class, or a checklist forms the basis for the discussion. A few guidelines will get you started on student conferences:

Let the student talk first.
Ask leading questions:

Which part of this piece are you happiest with? Why?
Which parts don't sound right? Can you explain that part to me in another way?
What things gave you trouble in this piece of writing?
How can I help you?

When you talk . . .
Keep it positive—"I like this part a lot." And be concrete—"I like the name you chose for the dog in your story."

Make suggestions, not criticisms. Suggestions focus on the positive—what can be done better—and they are just suggestions (that is, your point of view); they are not demands or orders. Suggestions leave the ownership of the next action with the writer, not with the teacher. Criticisms focus on what's wrong without giving any feedback about how the "mistake" can be corrected. When discussing a weak point in the writing, it is always a good idea to point to a place where the writer has done a good job. So, for example, a teacher might say, "I think your story would be more interesting if you described the trail more. Remember your last story—the one about the first time you made brownies? In that story I knew that your kitchen had coffeepots on the wallpaper. Can you tell me things like that about the trail so I can see it in my head like I could see the kitchen in my head?" This kind of suggestion is concrete—and it draws on something the writer has done well before.

Talk about the piece of writing, not about the writer. Say "Your story does a good job when it . . ." or "Your story would be stronger if it . . ." not "You did a good job," or "You need to improve . . ."

Stick to the things you're teaching at the moment (evaluating on) unless the student brings something else up.

Keep it short. Make suggestions; don't rewrite the student's work orally.

If the conference is being used to put a grade on a piece . . .

First, ask the student what grade he or she would give the piece, and why. Next, state what grade you think the piece should have and why. Finally, negotiate between your two positions if there is a difference.

Let's look at an example. In this situation Ms. O'Neil has asked her intermediate-level students to write a descriptive piece about an animal they like. Her instruction has focused on descriptive language and punctuation. She is using a primary-trait approach to evaluate the writing on those two items. Crystal brings the piece in Figure 5.1 to her conference with Ms. O'Neil. The conference goes like this:

Ms. O'Neil: Hi, Crystal. Are you ready to evaluate your descriptive piece?"

Crystal: It's a poem.

M: O.K. Let's take a look at it. Tell me what you wrote about.

C: Tigers.

M: Great. You like cats, don't you?

C: [Nods.]

M: O.K. This time we're working on descriptions and punctuation, right? Tell me what you think works well in your poem.

C: I like my descriptions. I think I told a lot about the tiger.

FIGURE 5.1. Crystal's Poem

The Tiger
The tiger is so quiet, its like a tree swaying in the wind
The tiger stalks its food, he is as quiet as a mouse.
The tiger sees the long tall grass sway as the creature walks through it
the tiger knows its prey is there
The tiger runs to catch its food, he's as fast as a race car.
The tiger pounces on its prey, its prey was a mouse

M: [Reads.] Yes. I agree. I especially like this description of the tiger being so quiet. What else?

C: My handwriting is smaller. I got more on the page.

M: That's right. Good. You've been working on your handwriting haven't you?

C: Yes. It doesn't look so babyish now.

M: Good. Anything you're not happy with about this poem?

C: I'm worried about punctuation. I think I wrote some run-on sentences.

M: What is a run-on sentence?

C: It's just I keep going and going. There should be a period, but I don't put it.

M: How do you find one?

C: I have to read back through it and when I run out of breath, I say, "Should there be a period? Yeah." I can't keep going. Because usually I just put a comma right after the subject. Like 'The beach was pretty, the seagulls flew,' no period between those, so I have to put one.

M: O.K. That's good. So show me a run-on sentence in your poem. I see a couple. Can you find them?

C: Maybe a period after "quiet."

M: Right. Do you see the next one?

C: After "food."

M: Good! There are two more. See if you can find them.

C: "The tiger runs to catch its food."

M: Did you learn about semicolons last year?

C: Yes. A comma with a dot over it.

M: Do you know what a semicolon means?

C: There's either a comma there or a period there or something.

M: [Nods.] It means a period ought to go here—that's what the dot is—but I want a comma to go here—that's what the comma is. And so it's strong enough to stand in the place of a period, but it still keeps it one sentence like a comma would. Like the first—a semicolon would be really good between "the tiger is so quiet" and "it's like a tree swaying in the wind." Can you tell me why?

C: Because it's all the same subject.

M: Exactly. The tiger is quiet and the tiger is like a tree.

C: Yeah.

M: Now tell me about the next one.

C: Well, "quiet as a mouse" tells how he stalks his food.

M: Exactly. And what about the last one. Would you put a period or a semicolon?

C: Well, I'd put a period.

M: I would too. How come?

C: Because the tiger pounces is one idea and the prey was a mouse is another idea.

M: Right. The tiger is the worker in this sentence. The mouse is the worker in the other one, so a period separates them into two sentences. That's good. Why don't you take your poem and fix all the run-ons?

C: O.K.

M: How do you think you'll feel about this poem once you're done with it?

C: I think it's pretty good. Maybe I'll put it in my portfolio.

M: Good idea.

Sometimes teachers use group conferences. If she had read the writing ahead of time and realized that several students were ready to learn about semicolons, Ms. O'Neil might have chosen to group three or four writers together for this conference rather than dealing only with Crystal. In situations where grades would be determined by the conference, however, group conferences are not a good idea.

Some Advantages of Writing Conferences

a. Students have a chance to explain what they did and give input into the evaluation.
b. Students get immediate explanations of the evaluation; these explanations offer on-the-spot teaching opportunities.
c. The teacher receives immediate feedback regarding his or her assessment of the student's writing; negotiation is possible.

Some Disadvantages of Writing Conferences

a. Conferences are time-consuming.
b. Negative confrontations sometimes occur. (Students can become emotional.)

Tape-recorded Responses

Tape-recorded responses are one-way "conferences" with students; teachers who use this method simply speak their responses into a tape recorder and provide an opportunity (and the equipment) for students to listen to the tape-recorded message. The guidelines are the same as for two-way conferences: be positive, be concrete, offer suggestions rather than criticisms, talk about the piece of writing rather than the writer, keep it short, and stick to what is being evaluated.

Some Advantages of Tape-recorded Responses

a. Students get an explanation of the grade with some revision tips.
b. Tape-recordings do not take as much time as face-to-face conferences.

Some Disadvantages of Tape-recorded Responses

a. They require a tape recorder, tapes, and a listening station.
b. The teacher does not get feedback from the student.

Now let's look at a scenario for using oral responses. Ms. Ratliff teaches sixth grade. For the most part, her students are enthusiastic writers. In the spring she teaches a unit on state history. She requires all of them to do a piece of writing, but she allows them to make choices about what kinds of things they want to write. Some of her students are working on research reports; some are writing tall tales; a few are writing letters to state legislators. The grading approach Ms. Ratliff is using is an analytic approach, assignment-generated rubrics (she has designed a rubric for the research report, another for a tall tale, a third for a letter). She decides to have conferences to grade the writing because the pieces are so highly individualized.

She schedules ten minutes for each conference. The first student she sees, Maureen, has written a research report about the wildflowers of the state. Ms. Ratliff gets out the research report rubric (which Ms. Ratliff had given to

Maureen when she chose her topic). She asks Maureen to tell her about her report by referring to the rubric. Maureen points out the strong points and the things that gave her trouble. Ms. Ratliff agrees with Maureen's analysis of her report. She makes a few suggestions for revision and they agree on a grade of "B." Ms. Ratliff suggests that Maureen revise her report according to their discussion and the rubric if she would like to have an "A."

Written Responses

Using the Computer

Teachers who work in a computer lab often compose written responses to their students at the end of the computer file containing the piece of writing being evaluated. Other teachers who have computers at home compose letters to students on their own word processors and print them out for distribution. The guidelines for these letters are similar to the guidelines for writing conferences and tape-recorded responses.

Handwritten Notes

Handwritten notes usually appear in three forms: Post-it notes positioned throughout the piece of writing, a code system of editor's marks throughout the piece, and comments at the end. Post-it notes have the advantage of leaving the writer's work intact. They can literally be removed and followed or ignored. The student writer retains ownership of the writing. Systems of editor's marks throughout the paper, while common in practice, rob students of ownership, are often confusing, and tend to focus on the negative. Comments at the end often get overlooked. Written notes should also follow the guidelines for writing conferences.

Grading Sheets

A grading sheet is usually a teacher-made form (often simply a copy of a rubric) designed to provide standardized responses to an entire class of writers. Grading sheets have the advantage of superimposing an appearance of standardization on grading. This is also their disadvantage.

Some Advantages of Written Responses
a. They provide a permanent record of teacher response.
b. They can be brief or lengthy, depending on need.
c. They can be made without the student being physically present.

Some Disadvantages of Written Responses
a. Traditionally they have focused on the negative.
b. They are often ignored or overlooked by students.

Now let's look at a scenario for using written responses for grading. Remember Mr. Martinez and his poems from cluster grading? Because he is pressed for class time (achievement testing is underway), he decides to respond to his fourth graders in writing. For example, he writes Tina a note on his home computer commenting on what he likes about her poem—the imagery. (Tina's poem was in the "✓" group.) He suggests that she read several poems by classmates (from the "+" group) if she wants to revise her poem.

Grades without Comments

Grades without comments communicate very little to students. However, in situations where students will not have their papers returned or where they will not revise, grades without comments get the job done very quickly. At other times during the year, however, they can be disappointing to students who have worked hard on their writing. Sometimes teachers choose to provide voluntary opportunities for students who would like in-depth response to accompany their grades. These students sign up for conferences to discuss their grades, but students who are happy with simply a grade are accommodated as well. The disadvantage to this approach is that often only a few students approach the teacher for comments.

Here is a possible scenario. Mr. Foster teaches third grade. In his school, students must write an end-of-the-year writing sample to pass along to their next year's teacher. Because the students do not get their papers back and they have no opportunity to revise, Mr. Foster simply put grades on the papers (with no response) and includes them in the last nine weeks' writing grade.

Chapter Summary

Teacher responses can be delivered orally by face-to-face conferences or by tape-recorded messages. They can also be delivered in written form by computer, Post-it-notes, a system of editor's marks, or comments at the end of the piece. Using any of these strategies, teacher responses should be positive and concrete, should focus on the piece of writing rather than on the writer, and should offer suggestions rather than criticisms.

EXERCISES

1. Think back to when you were an elementary school student. What method(s) did your teachers use to respond to your writing? List them. How did you feel about the teachers' responses to your writing? How much did you learn from your teachers' responses?

2. Think about the writing you do now. What kind of response is the most helpful to you? What kind is the least helpful?

3. Write brief anecdotes of the most helpful and least helpful responses you remember getting from a teacher about your writing. Share them with your group.

4. Imagine a scenario in which you, as a teacher, might use in a positive manner each of the response strategies described in this chapter. Imagine a scenario for other response strategies you are familiar with. Discuss these scenarios with your group.

CHAPTER 6

Management Systems

Management systems are options that teachers have for arriving at cumulative grades—grades for a nine-week grading period or for a year. This chapter discusses four management systems: traditional grade averaging and three less-traditional methods—checklists, contracts, and portfolios. Management systems are not grading approaches, nor are they response strategies, so both a grading approach and a response strategy will have to be superimposed upon a management system. For example, grades arrived at by some holistic measure can still be averaged in a traditional way or they can be grouped into a portfolio. They can be reported to students in conferences, on tapes, in notes, and so forth. Some grading approaches work better with some management systems than others, and some response strategies seem to "fit" better, but there are no hard-and-fast rules for matching a management system with grading approaches and response strategies—always there are choices, options. The context of the individual classroom is what drives the decisions. (This issue is discussed in depth in Part III.)

Grade Averaging

This traditional system assigns a mathematical value to a particular grade and computes an average mathematical score. The mathematical value is then reconverted to the appropriate grade. The process is often referred to as a common value system.

Common Value Systems

Common Value System #1
E (excellent) = above 85%
S (satisfactory) = between 85% and 70%
I (improving) = between 70% and 60%
N (needs to improve) = below 60%

For example, Mr. Johnson has decided on the following system: E = 95; E− = 87; S+ = 82; S = 78; S− = 72; I+ = 68; I = 65; I− = 62. If Teresa, a student in his class, has written four graded pieces with the grades of "E," "E," "S+," "S−," her nine-week grade might be calculated as below:

    95
    95
    82
    +72
    344   344 divided by 4 = 86

Teresa would receive an "E" for the nine weeks.

Common Value System #2

"+" = 80% or better
"✓" = between 80% and 50%
"−" = less than 50%

If, for example, Tony had done five pieces of writing on which he had received three grades of "+" and two grades of "✓," Ms. Brewer might average his grade like this: 90 + 90 + 90 + 70 + 70 = 410. Since 410 divided by 5 is 82, Tony would receive a "+" for the nine weeks.

Common Value System #3

A = 90%
B = 89%–80%
C = 79%–70%
D = 69%–60%
F = 59%—

If Angela had done seven pieces of graded writing in the nine weeks, and had received grades of "C−," "D+," "C+," "B−," "C," "C−," "C," Mrs. Avery might average her grade like this: 72 + 68 + 78 + 82 + 75 + 72 + 75 = 522. Since 522 divided by 7 is 74.6, Angela would receive a grade of "C" for the nine weeks.

Variations of Grade Averaging

Point systems. Rather than using a letter grade at all, a teacher may assign points to a piece of writing in the first place. So, for example a "+" may be assigned a "3," a "✓" may be assigned a "2," and a "−" may be assigned a "1." In this variation, Tony's grade (common value system #2 above) would look like this: 3 + 3 + 3 + 2 + 2 = 13. Thirteen divided by 5 = 2.6, so Tony would receive a "+" for the nine weeks.

Grade weighting. Rather than weighting each assignment equally, a teacher may assign different point values to various pieces of writing. So, for example, the first piece of writing might be worth 50 points, the second two might be worth 75 points, and the last worth 100 points, even though the assignments were of about the same length. This variation assumes growth on the part of students as time goes by. In this variation, Teresa's grade (common value system #1 above) might look like this:

E (.95 × 50) 48
E (.95 × 75) 71
S+ (.82 × 75) 62
S− (.72 × 100) 72
                253

Since there are 300 points possible, her nine-week grade would be 253 divided by 300, or 84. She would receive an "S."

In all three of the sample value systems, the teachers will still impose a grading approach. For example, Mr. Johnson grades Teresa's writing holistically against anchor papers provided by his district. Ms. Brewer grades Tony's writing with questions for grading, and Mrs. Avery creates rubrics for each individual assignment. Likewise, they all use different response strategies. Mr. Johnson tapes his responses to Angela, Ms. Brewer gives Tony a grading sheet based on the questions, and Mrs. Avery attaches Post-it-note comments throughout Andrea's writing.

Some Advantages of Grade Averaging

a. This is a traditional method of arriving at grades, used in most subject areas. It is familiar.
b. Final grades are easy to "defend" using this system. The math involved provides a sense of objectivity to a long-term grade.

Some Disadvantages of Grade Averaging

a. Converting letter grades to numbers and back again is a statistically unsound procedure. Letter grades divide student work into three to five categories. Percentages assume 100 categories. Arbitrarily assigning a percentage to a letter so that the letters can be "added up" leads to relatively meaningless final grades.
b. As the example of Teresa shows, final grades can vary depending on how points are assigned by the teacher.

Checklists and Cumulative Records

Checklists provide a cumulative record of student achievement. They allow a teacher to track the progress of individual students and see at a glance which parts of the writing puzzle have been mastered and which parts need more work. Final grades can be determined based on cumulative performance rather than on the success of any single piece of writing. Figure 6.1 is an example of a checklist for second-grade writing.

FIGURE 6.1. Sample Checklist

Student's Name _____   Beginning Date _____

Ending Date _____

Writing Assignment	1	2	3	4	5	6

I. CONTEXT CONCEPTS
identifies purpose of the writing

expresses personal satisfaction with own writing

II. CONTENT CONCEPTS
main idea is clear

completes ideas

eliminates content gaps

includes details to support the main idea

III. STRUCTURE CONCEPTS
writing contains a beginning, a middle, and an end

details are sequenced logically

personal experience narrative successfully completed

imaginative story successfully completed

report based on personal observation successfully completed

letter successfully completed

IV. MECHANICS—The final draft illustrates:
sentences containing a complete thought

transitions and conjunctions to connect ideas

conventional word endings

personal pronouns used correctly

contractions used correctly

singular possessives used correctly

verb tenses used correctly

subject-verb agreement

conventional spelling

proper punctuation

correct use of capital letters

FIGURE 6.1. Sample Checklist (continued)

Writing Assignment	1	2	3	4	5	6
V. PROCESS CONCEPTS						
successfully prewrites						
writes a rough draft						
participates in revising						
participates in editing						
writes a final draft						
shares writing with an audience						

Mr. Starner is a second-grade teacher who uses the checklist in Figure 6.1. Andrea is a student in his class. As Andrea turns in her pieces of writing, Mr. Starner records her successes on the checklist. A "✓" in a box lets him know that Andrea has successfully used the item identified. The first two sections of Andrea's checklist are illustrated in Figure 6.2.

At the end of the nine weeks, Mr. Starner knows that Andrea has successfully completed five out of the six items on these first two sections of the checklist. Her writing still contains content gaps, and she has only recently

FIGURE 6.2. Partial Checklist Filled Out

	Writing Assignment					
	1	2	3	4	5	6
I. CONTEXT CONCEPTS						
identifies purpose of the writing						✓
expresses personal satisfaction with own writing		✓				
II. CONTENT CONCEPTS						
main idea is clear					✓	
completes ideas	✓					
eliminates content gaps						
includes details to support the main idea	✓					

demonstrated a grasp of purpose in her writing, but she has enjoyed her own writing from the first, and it is filled with details. Mr. Starner examines the rest of the checklist in the same way. To arrive at a grade, however, he must impose a grading approach on his management system. Because a checklist is analytic in nature he will probably choose an analytic approach. This particular checklist is based on an exhaustive list of criteria, so Mr. Starner will probably choose a criterion-referenced approach and simply assign points to each category on his checklist and add up Andrea's grade.

But checklists can be used with other approaches as well. A primary-trait checklist can be created, for example. Or the checklists from a whole class may be graded using a cluster holistic method (one stack of the best checklists, a second of the weakest, a third of those in between, etc.). Or a grade-level committee might choose anchor checklists for various grades, and teachers might compare individual student checklists with the anchor profile.

Mr. Starner will also need to choose a response strategy. For example, he may schedule a conference with Andrea to discuss her checklist with her and to suggest things she might like to focus on for the next nine weeks, or he may give Andrea her checklist with its grade at the top (grade with no response), or he may write her a note, and so forth.

Some Advantages of Checklists
a. They provide a cumulative record of particular skills students have mastered.
b. They show clearly which skills a student needs to continue to work on.

Some Disadvantages of Checklists
a. They assume that if a student can master a particular list of skills, his or her writing will be good.
b. They superimpose an assumption that each item on the checklist is of equal value, while in reality understanding the context of a piece of writing may be far more important to its success than having every word spelled correctly.

Contracts

This management system allows students to choose how much (and sometimes what type of) work they wish to do. Grades are attached to work that is completed at a specified level of acceptability. Individual pieces of writing are evaluated simply by the words "accepted," "needs to be redone," or "not done." While at first glance this management system may appear to be an exception to the grade-approach rule, in reality a grade approach will still be superimposed on a contract. A contract may be analytic or holistic: it may be based on completion of primary-trait criteria, for example, or on successful illustration of different forms of writing ("successful" being judged holistically). In this management system, however, individual grades are not accumulated. The long-term grade is determined by the fulfillment (or lack of fulfillment) of the contract.

A sample will illustrate. The contract in Figure 6.3 might be used by Mr. Adler in an intermediate classroom for a unit on expository writing.

This contract is an example of a primary-trait contract. For "N" the trait is simply completion of the assignments. For "I" the traits are completion, organization, and general surface-level accuracy. For "S" the traits are completion, organization, accuracy, and process participation. For "E" the traits are the same as for "S" but there is one more piece of writing required. If Mr. Adler

---

FIGURE 6.3. Sample Contract

STUDENT'S NAME _____ Beginning Date _____

Ending Date _____

For a grade of "N" (needs improvement), the student will write

1. directions for completing a process (working a jigsaw puzzle, changing a bicycle tire, giving a home permanent, etc.)
2. an explanation of a point of view (why Christmas is your favorite time of year, why you hate baseball, why gerbils make good pets, etc.)
3. a summary (of a book you've read, of three encyclopedia articles on the same topic, of December's newspaper reports on the drought, etc.)

For a grade of "I" (improving), the student will complete the requirements for "N," but essays will be

a. clearly organized with main idea statements and paragraph topic sentences
b. be largely free of mechanical errors

For a grade of "S" (satisfactory), the student will complete the requirements for "I" and show evidence of the writing process:

a. turn in prewriting and at least two different drafts
b. participate in peer revision and editing groups
c. share the final drafts with an audience

For a grade of "E" (excellent), the student will complete the requirements for "S" as well as write one more essay:

a comparison/contrast essay (how sixth grade is different and how it is the same as fifth grade, how pet dogs are different and how they are the same as pet cats, how the movie is the same as the book *Old Yeller*, etc.)

---

grades his students using this contract, he will still have to choose a response strategy. Will he have conferences? Will he write a letter to each student? Or will he choose not to comment at all?

Some Advantages of Contracts
a. They reduce the decision making (and therefore the pressure) of final grades.
b. Students know exactly what kind of and how much work is required for a particular grade.
c. They allow students to make choices about what grade they wish to work for, providing students who are not particularly interested in writing an opportunity to focus their energy in channels of their own choosing.

Some Disadvantages of Contracts
a. Not all students fall neatly into contract packages. Teachers are left to negotiate grades with those students who fulfill the requirements of a particular grade but do so with marginal quality.
b. Students with low self-images may opt to work for a lower grade than they are actually capable of achieving, simply out a lack of self-confidence.

Portfolios

In this management system, only selected pieces of completed student writing are graded. Students make choices about which pieces of writing they wish to submit for a grade. Thus, two distinct collections of student work exist in the classroom: a writing folder containing all student work, including work-in-progress, and a portfolio containing examples of the student's best work. Like contracts, portfolios may be analytic or holistic. Portfolios that are graded with reference to a list of skills demonstrated might be thought of as "criterion-referenced portfolios." Portfolios that are graded with reference to anchors or with reference to the other portfolios developed in the classroom might be thought of as "holistic portfolios." It is possible to create a set of questions to use as a grading approach with portfolios, or a short list of primary-traits. In fact, portfolios can be developed using any of the grading approaches.

An example will illustrate. Mrs. Ford has organized her fifth-graders' writing into a portfolio system. Her curriculum guide requires her to teach the following types of writing over the course of the year:

personal narrative
friendly letter
business letter

description
directions
explanation
summary
comparison and contrast
persuasive writing
the short story
poetry

She divides these types of writing into four units: self-expressive writing (personal narrative and friendly letter); expository writing (business letter, directions, explanation, summary, comparison and contrast); persuasive writing; and literary writing (description, short story, and poetry). Within each unit she makes three or four writing assignments, all of which go into the students' writing folders. At the end of each unit, she instructs her students to select the one assignment they consider shows their best writing from that unit. These pieces are then revised and edited with peer help and placed in their portfolios. At the end of the year, each student has a portfolio containing four pieces of excellent writing—one for each unit. If Mrs. Ford wishes to grade the pieces of writing as the year goes along, she must determine whether she will use an analytic or a holistic approach. If she wishes to look at the portfolios as entities, she must decide whether she wishes to look at them holistically (clusters of portfolios or anchor portfolios), or if she wishes to look at them analytically (primary traits of "E" portfolios, for example, or a list of criteria that "A" portfolios must meet).

As with the other management systems, Mrs. Ford will choose a response strategy. Conferences seem a natural companion for portfolios, but certain factors in the instructional context may make other choices appropriate as well.

Some Advantages of Portfolios
a. They can dramatically decrease the pressure of grades on students, thus providing an environment conducive to risk-taking and real learning.
b. They can allow students to participate in the grading process by choosing which pieces they wish to have graded.
c. They can decrease the pressure of grades on the teacher as well because grading occurs much less frequently.

Some Disadvantages of Portfolios
a. Some students are uneasy receiving grades only periodically. They continually ask for reassurance—"How am I doing, teacher?"
b. The paper load may increase at grading time. The teacher may be faced with evaluating four or five papers per student at one time rather than seeing one paper at a time over a term.

Chapter Summary

Management systems provide options for teachers in determining long-range grades. While grade averaging is the traditional management system, checklists, contracts, and portfolios offer alternative methods of arriving at nine-week or year-end grades. Each management system will be accompanied by a grading approach—analytic or holistic—and a response strategy—oral, written, or no comment.

EXERCISES

1. Create a holistic contract.

2. Create a rubric for grading a primary portfolio.

3. Which of the four management systems described in this chapter have you experienced as a student? as a teacher? Add to the lists of advantages and disadvantages for those systems.

4. Which of these four management systems is new to you? Describe a situation in which you think that system might be useful.

5. What local political ramifications of these four management systems might you have to cope with? (How are they viewed by power groups in your school district?)

CHAPTER 7

Evaluation Styles

Evaluation styles are options teachers have for centering the power of the decisions. The power for the decisions may reside with the teacher (the traditional approach); it may reside with the student (self-evaluation) or with peers (student-centered); it may reside with all three (teacher/student partnerships); or it may reside outside the classroom (school or district guidelines).

Teacher-centered Evaluation

Teacher-centered grading is the traditional evaluation style. In this style, teachers set grading standards, evaluate student work against those standards, and assign grades. Teacher-centered evaluation can occur not only with traditional grading techniques such as analytic grading, comments at the end of a paper, and grade averaging, but also with less traditional approaches, responses, and management systems.

For example, following a teacher-centered evaluation style, using an assignment-generated criteria approach, Mr. Thomas would design a rubric for a personal narrative assignment and share that rubric with his students, explaining to them what he thinks makes a strong piece of personal writing. The students would write their papers and turn them in to him; Mr. Thomas would compare each paper to his rubric and assign a grade. He might tape-record his responses to his students and provide a listening station for them. He might average their grades at the end of the nine weeks, or he might collect their best work in a portfolio to send home to parents.

Some Advantages of Teacher-centered Evaluation
a. As the most knowledgeable person in the class, the teacher retains control of the evaluation criteria (and thus the instructional goals).
b. Because this is the traditional evaluation style, most parents and students are comfortable with it.

Some Disadvantages of Teacher-centered Evaluation
a. Classrooms often become autocratic when this evaluation style is used exclusively.
b. Most students, especially as they get older, are not as concerned about the teacher's criteria for evaluation as they are about their peers'.

Self-evaluation

Self-evaluation of work is implicit in the choices for portfolios, but self-evaluation can be used with other grading techniques as well. In self-evaluation the student writer makes evaluation decisions. The student writer may choose the form of the piece of writing, research it, and draw up a rubric against which he or she plans to evaluate the final draft. Or the student writer may compare the piece of writing against a checklist of criteria. The student writer may state an appropriate grade for the portfolio and write a letter defending that decision.

Let's look at an example. Miss Benjamin teaches second grade. Above all she wants her students to become independent workers. She decides to have her students use a self-evaluation style. She chooses a primary-trait grading approach, a written response strategy, and a checklist management system.

First, Miss Benjamin teaches personal writing to her students. She creates a checklist of the different types of personal writing her students must complete before the end of the unit. She reads them letters and stories written in the first person; she has them tell personal stories to small groups; and she shares pieces of her own personal writing with the class. Next, she asks each of her students to choose one type of writing from the checklist. Once they have chosen, they each make a list of the three things they like best in that type of writing. They then write a piece using that form.

After her students have completed the final drafts of their personal pieces, Miss Benjamin asks them to compare their own writing against their lists of things they liked. She asks them to write her a letter telling her how they think their own writing compared to their lists and check the piece off on the checklist.

Self-evaluation occurs whenever student writers set their own goals and compare their work against these goals. It may also play a part in other grading techniques such as writing conferences. For example, students may be asked open-ended questions that call for evaluative decisions: what was hardest about this piece? what did you do better today? Writers' journals may include self-evaluation: after each assignment the student may be asked to write a journal entry answering open-ended, evaluative questions.

Some Advantages of Self-evaluation
a. Students internalize criteria when they generate them.
b. Competition is against the self only.
c. Students take charge of their own progress.

Some Disadvantages of Self-evaluation

a. Students may overlook some important pieces of the writing puzzle, resulting in "practicing their oversights."

b. Students who are not self-starters may be uncomfortable with self-evaluation.

c. Administrators may need to be educated about how this evaluation style works.

d. Parents may need to be educated about the advantages of this evaluation style.

Peer-centered Evaluation

Peer-centered grading depends on the class for criteria, evaluation, and grades. In this style, students cooperatively set the standards for writing assignments; they evaluate one another's work; and they assign grades to each other. For example, in the same class cited in Mr. Thomas's class (in teacher-centered evaluation above), instead of working from Mr. Thomas's definition of good personal writing, the class would discuss the criteria of good personal writing, based on their experiences. They would then create a class rubric and write their papers. Then teams of students (perhaps peer revision groups) would read the papers, compare them to the class-generated rubric, and assign grades to each other.

Some Advantages of Peer-centered Evaluation

a. Students internalize criteria when they generate them.

b. Students learn from each other's work when they evaluate their peers' writing.

Some Disadvantages of Peer-centered Evaluation

a. Students do not possess the training and experience teachers have for setting criteria.

b. Students are sometimes unreasonably hard on each other.

c. Administrators may need to be educated about how this evaluation style works.

d. Parents may need to be educated about the advantages of this evaluation style.

Teacher/Student Partnerships

This evaluation style depends on student input as well as teacher guidance. A teacher may lead a discussion in which the class adds input to grading criteria or creates a rubric or a checklist. In a conference, the teacher may work with an individual student to set personal writing goals for the next assignment. Individual or group contracts might be designed with both teacher and student input. The variation is endless. The common theme is input from both sides of the teacher's desk.

For example, Mr. Thomas might discuss the characteristics of good personal writing with his class. On the board they might together design a rubric that contained some characteristics of good personal writing suggested by the students and some suggested by Mr. Thomas. Together they would negotiate the final form of the evaluation rubric. The students would write their papers, help one another revise according to the rubric, and turn their papers in. At that point Mr. Thomas might evaluate the papers against the class rubric and assign grades; he might have students do self-evaluations based on the rubric; he might have peer groups evaluate each other's papers; or he might do something else in a teacher/student combination.

Some Advantages of Teacher/Student Partnerships
a. Students invest in grades that they feel they have had input to.
b. Students learn to think critically about writing by being involved in the evaluation process.
c. Teachers become sensitive to what their students consider good writing.

Some Disadvantages of Teacher/Student Partnerships
a. Administrators may need to be educated about how this evaluation style works.
b. Parents may need to be educated about the advantages of this evaluation style.

Outside the Classroom

This evaluation style depends on an outside authority to set evaluation criteria and standards. Most often the outside authority is represented by a set of guidelines, a rubric, or an anchor provided by a grade-level committee, a school, or a district. In this style, teachers are expected to conform with standards created by someone else or agreed on by a majority vote. Approaches, response strategies, and management systems may be dictated as well, or they may be left up to the individual teacher's choice.

In this system, new teachers are trained in the agreed-upon criteria and expected to follow the guidelines used by everyone else. Sometimes evaluation is conducted by teams of teachers grading the writing of each other's students, rather than being left to the classroom teacher. In this way, then, instruction and evaluation may become divergent, or evaluation criteria may drive instruction.

Some Advantages of Outside Authority

a. Teamwork among writing teachers develops, often leading to frequent interchange about goals of instruction and criteria for particular grades.

b. Students (and parents) who remain in this school soon learn "what is expected."

Some Disadvantages of Outside Authority

a. Guidelines imposed from outside make it virtually impossible for a classroom teacher to match his or her instructional purposes to a particular student audience, unless the teacher chooses to ignore evaluation criteria when designing lessons.

b. Outside authority is often out of step with current practice—either outstripping it in an effort to force change or lagging behind it and not allowing change.

Chapter Summary

Evaluation styles determine where the power for the decision-making in grading resides. If the power resides with the teacher, we call the evaluation style "teacher-centered." If the power resides with the student writer, we call the evaluation style "self-evaluation." If the class makes grading decisions, the style is "peer-centered." A combination of any of these styles results in a "teacher/student partnership." Occasionally the power may reside in an outside authority.

EXERCISES

1. Discuss the power issues of evaluation styles.

2. Where on this continuum

Teacher	Partners	Students

have you encountered grades—as a student? as a teacher?

3. In what kind of evaluation style are you most comfortable as a student? why?

4. as a teacher? why?

CHAPTER 8

Hybrids

Most often teachers choose from among the evaluation options and design their own systems using a combination of techniques. For example, it is possible to begin with primary-trait grading and gradually add traits until by the end of the year a criterion-referenced approach has been arrived at. Or it is possible to use student-generated rubrics from which the teacher grades or teacher-generated rubrics from which the students evaluate each other's work. Or a contract may specify particular inclusions in an end-of-the-year portfolio. A rubric may be created from anchor papers. A group of portfolios may be graded using a "cluster" holistic method (one stack of excellent portfolios, a second stack of weak portfolios, a third stack of in-between portfolios, and so forth). Anchor portfolios can be created at a particular grade level, or a checklist may dictate the entries in a portfolio. The number of combinations and hybrids seems infinite.

Let's take an example. Mrs. Ford (from the portfolio example in Chapter 6) makes a checklist from the pieces of writing she is expected to teach in fifth grade. She places this checklist in student work folders. At the end of each unit (personal, expository, persuasive, and literary), she has her students check off the items in their work folders that have been completed and place their best piece in a portfolio. Each nine weeks she examines the students' checklists and arrives at a grade using a point system per item included. At the end of the year, each student has a portfolio containing four pieces of writing—a personal piece, an expository piece, a persuasive piece, and a literary piece. Mrs. Ford grades the portfolios using a cluster holistic method. She arrives at a final grade by averaging the checklist grades and the portfolio grade.

Of course it is possible to create negative hybrids. For example, sometimes primary-trait written comments are stuck on to the end of a paper to justify an impressionistic "holistic" grade. This system is a negative hybrid because unstated primary traits are little more than momentary teacher reactions.

Sometimes large-scale writing assessments are hybrid systems. The Arizona Student Assessment Program from which the anchors in Chapter 4 are drawn is actually a hybrid system. Anchors (holistic) are provided to the scorers along with primary-trait rubrics (analytic). Student writing is scored holistically with reference to the anchor papers. The analytic rubrics are used as a back-up for confusing cases. There are two grading observations: one for content and structure, a second for grammar and mechanics, resulting in a primary-trait evaluation. Figures 8.1 and 8.2 present the rubrics that are used with the anchors.

Chapter Summary

Hybrids are grading systems that are made up of more than one approach, response strategy, management system, or evaluation style. In the real world of teaching hybrids are the rule, not the exception.

FIGURE 8.1. Rubric 1

RUBRIC FOR OBSERVATION 1 (3W-5A)

Note: Evaluate how effectively and appropriately each writer presents ideas and uses the specified form (e.g., short story, poem, report, critique). As much as possible, scorers should at this time disregard conventions of writing (e.g., formats, capitalization, spelling, punctuation, and paragraphing). Poems should generally be five to ten lines long, but longer or shorter poems may be acceptable if they are skillfully organized and complete. It is not necessary for a poem to rhyme.

A 4 poem fully describes the child's toy. It uses descriptive details based on the five senses to illustrate and enliven the subject. The poem appears in lines rather than run-on sentences, and the lines are arranged in a pattern.

A 3 poem calls on the five senses to describe a toy. However, this description may not be creative or specific enough to fully describe and enliven the subject. The poem appears in lines, and the lines are arranged in a pattern.

A 2 poem lacks the forms or patterns normally associated with poetry and may rely on sentences and/or paragraph forms rather than lines or stanzas. The writer describes a toy, but refers to few sensory details.

A 1 poem is not a poem. It contains none of the patterns and forms associated with poetry, and it only briefly mentions the toy.

A 0 should be assigned if the student has failed to attempt the poem.

An N/S (nonscorable) should be assigned if the poem is illegible or unreadable. This includes poems written in a language other than English.

FIGURE 8.2. Rubric 2

RUBRIC FOR OBSERVATION 2 (3W-5A)

A 4 poem is easy to read. It is carefully proofread to correct spelling, usage, and grammar errors.

A 3 poem is generally well proofread, but it has occasional minor lapses in spelling, usage, and grammar.

A 2 poem is characterized by patterns of misspellings and/or serious usage flaws. It is somewhat difficult to follow and understand.

A 1 poem is poorly presented. It has a significant number of grammar or punctuation errors, sentence fragments, and/or flaws in usage. Almost every line contains an error.

A 0 should be assigned if the student has failed to attempt the poem.

An N/S (nonscorable) should be assigned if the poem is illegible or unreadable. This includes poems written in a language other than English.

EXERCISES

1. Create a primary-trait checklist. Specify the instructional purpose and the level of the student.

2. Choose a student paper from the Appendix. Fill out the checklist you created in Exercise 1 for that paper.

3. Create a contract from the checklist you created in Exercise 1.

4. Go back to the anchor papers your group chose for Exercise 6 in Chapter 4. Create rubrics from those papers.

5. Using either your own curriculum guide or the sample offered in Chapter 3, create a sample portfolio profile for primary writing.

6. Contact an elementary student. Ask him or her to tell you about a book he or she is reading. With the student's help, create a grading rubric for a book report he or she might write about this book.

PART III
Using Grading as a Teaching Tool

The first two parts of this book offer objectives and options for evaluating children's writing. But there remain questions larger than merely what tools are available for what purposes. These larger questions are: How to match a particular option with a particular purpose? How to learn to grade? How to use grading for more than arriving at "fair marks"? This part addresses these questions.

CHAPTER 9

Tools of the Trade
Choosing Evaluation Options in a Communication Setting

Using the Communication Triangle

As you think about how to choose from among the many evaluation options, you may want to review the communication triangle introduced in Chapter 2. For convenience, it is repeated here as Figure 9.1.

Next, let's review the grading options presented in this book: approaches, response strategies, management systems, and evaluation styles.

Any grading system we create will employ some choice in each of these categories. But too often we confuse the categories or overlook a category. When that happens, we lose our intentionality and often fall back on grading systems that our teachers used to grade us. (The traditional system, as most of us experienced it, consisted of teacher-centered analytic grading with no response, or brief—usually negative—comments written at the end of the paper. Grade averaging was the management system.) If we give up our intentionality, it is possible to find ourselves using a self-contradictory system of grading. The consequences of this self-contradiction can even affect instruction since grading often drives instruction and student learning.

An example will illustrate. Ms. McMillan attends a workshop on portfolios. She leaves the workshop enthusiastic about promoting student ownership of writing in her class, so she implements a portfolio management system. However, without thinking, she retains her traditional teacher-centered evaluation style: she dictates to the students what will go in their portfolios and the criteria upon which she will grade them. Without realizing it, Ms. McMillan has created a self-contradictory system: the evaluation style undercuts the instructional purpose of her management system. By dictating to her students what will go in their portfolios and what will make a good portfolio, she has actually retained ownership of her students' writing herself.

FIGURE 9.1. Communication Triangle

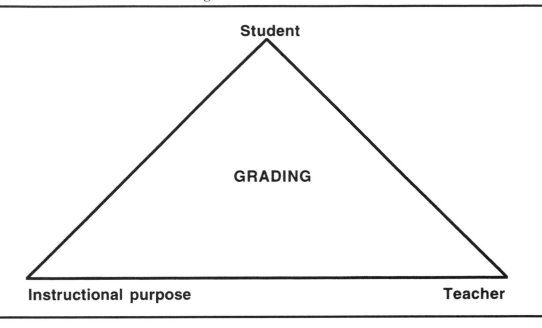

In order to avoid the trap of self-contradictory grading and instructional systems, we must always keep the communication triangle in mind. For it is in the interaction of the three corners of the triangle that we can make sensible, intentional decisions. Which corner we begin with cannot be prescribed—it is driven by the moment, by the context in which we find ourselves. The three scenarios that follow illustrate.

Scenario #1

Mr. Jaramillio's second-grade class is large and boisterous. By the end of the first week of school he knows he has a challenge on his hands. Some of his students are enthusiastic about writing, but some are fearful (they seem especially tense about spelling). Since he is a new second-grade teacher whose student teaching experience was in a fifth-grade classroom in another state, he is a bit unsure of what primary writers can do. He likes to write himself and wants to protect the enthusiasm for writing that some of his students possess as well as help the fearful students to feel more comfortable with writing. He wants to challenge them to develop as writers, and he wants to give them ownership of their writing. He thinks the best way to do this is to focus on writing for an audience, an unfamiliar concept to most of his students. Because his students are natural-born performers he counts on channeling this energy into writing.

Let's analyze Mr. Jaramillio's situation beginning at the "student" corner of the communication triangle:

Students: large, hard-to-control class; some enthusiastic writers, some fearful writers
Teacher: new at his job; likes to write
Instructional purpose(s): engender enthusiasm for and ownership of writing; focus on audience-awareness

Mr. Jaramillio makes the following choices:

Grading approach: primary-trait
Evaluation style: teacher-based
Response strategy: written (sticky pads)
Management system: contracts

Why did he make these decisions?

He has chosen a primary-trait approach because his two instructional goals look at pieces of writing as wholes—how kids feel about writing and how audiences respond to their writing.

He has chosen a teacher-based style for two reasons—because his students are largely unaware of what it means to write for someone other than themselves or their teachers and because of the control problems he is experiencing. He feels that until he achieves more decorum he needs to simply tell his students what he expects from their writing.

Because of his desire to develop student ownership of writing, he wants his response to be as unobtrusive as possible. He has decided to use brief written notes positioned on sticky paper at places in the writing where he wants to praise or make a suggestion. Using this method, students will see graphically that the writing is still their own, in spite of his comments.

He is enthusiastic about writing and he wants his students to feel the same way. He wants to avoid grades as much as possible. He has chosen a contract system to emphasize for his students that they can all get "+s." The contract spells out exactly how they can do this.

Scenario #2

Mrs. Begay has been teaching fourth grade for twenty years. She has always felt that writing was important and has had high standards for her students' work. She has taught from a traditional curriculum guide in traditional units: grammar, spelling, paragraphs, and so forth. But now she is ready for a change. She has been attending workshops and reading about holistic grading and is interested in trying it. Her students know her by reputation from their older brothers and sisters and expect a traditional approach, but some of them are familiar with portfolios because two of the third-grade teachers in the school use a portfolio system. In one of the workshops she attended, Mrs. Begay started keeping a personal journal. She has been surprised at how much she has enjoyed starting to write again after so many years of teaching writing but not writing herself. In fact, she is thinking about writing a collection of stories for her students. This year she wants to get away from the constant pressure of grades, both for herself and for her students. She wants her students to discover writing for themselves as she so recently has. She wants them to look at writing as a whole and as a process.

Let's analyze Mrs. Begay's situation beginning at the "teacher" corner of the communication triangle:

> *Teacher:* highly experienced but making a change in her philosophy of teaching writing; wants to get away from the constant pressure of grades
>
> *Students:* expect a traditional approach, but some of them have experience with portfolios
>
> *Instructional purpose(s):* help students relax with writing and discover the fun of it; help them view writing as a whole and as a process

Mrs. Begay makes the following choices:

> *Management system:* portfolios
> *Evaluation style:* partnership
> *Response strategy:* combination of oral and written
> *Grading approach:* holistic cluster

Let's look at why she made these decisions.

Since Mrs. Begay wants to avoid the constant pressure of grades for herself and for her students, she has chosen to use portfolios to determine nine-week grades. The portfolios will allow her to focus with her students on their progress, rather than on pieces of the puzzle isolated from each other as she has in the past. Because she wants her students to view writing as a whole rather than as the sum of its parts, Mrs. Begay has chosen a holistic method. She is comfortable with a cluster approach because of her years of experience with fourth-grade writing.

But, because Mrs. Begay will only assign grades at the end of each nine weeks, she has chosen a combination response strategy based on a partnership evaluation style. She plans to have conferences with her students about each one of their writing assignments and then provide them with evaluation guidelines to help them choose which of these assignments they will put in their portfolios. She will also have her students do a written evaluation of their portfolios after assembling them. Her evaluation of the portfolios will also be written, but she will schedule conferences with students who wish to discuss their portfolios with her. She hopes all of them will take advantage of this opportunity, but she does not wish to require these conferences because she will require assignment conferences.

Scenario #3

Ms. Paxton is an experienced teacher who has been teaching third grade for four years in a K–6 school. She has asked for and has been given a transfer to sixth grade. Because her students will be going to a junior high next year, she has spent several hours talking to the three seventh-grade English teachers. As a result of these conversations, she wants her students to get a conscious knowledge of all of the pieces of the writing puzzle. She also wants them to be able to articulate clearly what parts of their writing are well under control and what parts they need to continue to work on. However, since she is making a switch in level of student, she is a bit unsure of reasonable criteria for sixth-graders. She already knows some of her students from three years before, but many of the others are completely unknown to her. She wants to avoid making her "new" students feel less welcome than her "old" students.

Let's analyze Ms. Paxton's situation:

Instructional purpose(s): raise the pieces of the writing puzzle to a conscious level for the students; enable students to articulate what they do well in writing and what they need to work more on
Teacher: experienced but in a new setting; unsure of her expectations for this group of students
Students: sixth graders who are preparing for junior high, a new level of their education; a mix of kids she knows and kids she doesn't

To begin the year Ms. Paxton makes the following choices:

Grading approach: analytic
Evaluation style: peer-centered
Response strategy: oral
Management system: checklist

Let's look at why she made these decisions.

Because her instructional purposes call for students to be able to articulate the pieces of the writing puzzle, both in general and personal terms, she has chosen an analytic approach. A holistic approach would group students into "strong writers" and "weak writers," but it would not focus on the pieces of the puzzle. The checklist management system will support the analytic approach she has decided on as well as her second instructional purpose—to help her students get to know their strengths and weaknesses as writers.

She has chosen a partnership evaluation style because of the situation in which she finds herself: she is unsure of reasonable expectations for sixth-graders. Because she wants to get to know her "new" students quickly and because she wants to renew her acquaintance with her "old" students, she has chosen to respond to their writing orally, face-to-face, in conferences.

But let's follow Ms. Paxton through the year. She makes different choices as her situation changes. This is how the year progresses:

Ms. Paxton decides to begin her students writing using a personal experience narrative. It is required by the curriculum guide and she is familiar with it from teaching her third-graders. In a class discussion, she asks the students what they think makes a good personal narrative. Based on what they have said, she creates a primary-trait rubric for the personal narrative. The students write their papers following their rubrics, and she reads them. In individual conferences she discusses with the students how they assess the quality of their writing based on the class rubric. In the conferences, she arrives at a grade.

By January, Ms. Paxton begins to get some confidence. She moves from the student-based style to a partnership style. In this setting, she begins to add criteria to the class-generated rubrics. Because she feels comfortable with her students and confident that they will all approach her if they need to, she begins to tape-record her responses. As she reads a student's paper, she tapes her own evaluation of the quality of the writing based on the rubric. She creates a checklist in order to begin a cumulative record of how each student is progressing on the criteria she and the class have chosen up to this point.

By spring, Ms. Paxton has developed a criterion-referenced grading sheet from the checklist. She discusses junior high English classes with her students and moves into written responses based on her criterion-referenced grading sheet. She reinstitutes conferences: using the grading sheets, she discusses with her students which parts of their writing they feel are working well and which parts they think need more work. She calculates the last nine-week grades from the criterion-referenced checklist she has created.

In this scenario Ms. Paxton has used her grading system to support her instructional goals and to support herself as she gets to know a new teaching situation. She has balanced her students' perceived needs as writers with the needs she perceives them to have for the next level of their education. She has developed a flexible system that has allowed her instructional goals to develop.

Tools of the Trade

My suggested approach to evaluation—as decision making based on a communication context—views grading options as tools designed to serve instruction. It has been my experience that none of these options for grading is inherently "good" or "bad," just as a hammer or a pair of scissors is not inherently "good" or "bad." The "goodness" or "badness" depends on how the tool is used. A hammer that is used to build a church is a "good" hammer, while a hammer that is used to destroy an art object is a "bad" hammer. Therefore, I suggest that we use the metaphor of a toolbox as we think about matching grading strategy with instructional purpose. We have a toolbox full of tools: it is up to us to determine the shape of the job before us and choose appropriate tools. If I need to shorten a piece of molding, I need a saw, not a screwdriver. But if I need to tighten the leg on a couch, a screwdriver is exactly what I need.

And so it is for instructional jobs. Analytic grading is a useful tool for isolating problem areas and working to improve them. Anchor holistic grading is a useful tool for arriving at quick, accurate categories for large numbers of writers. Cluster holistic scoring is a tool that is useful for arriving at a quick, accurate profile of one class of student writers. Teacher-generated rubrics are useful for challenging students who need a better understanding of writing. Student-generated rubrics are useful for engendering student ownership of writing. Conferencing is a useful tool for building a writing-mentor relationship between a teacher and a student. Grades without comments are useful for final papers that will never be handed back or revised. A contract is a good tool for relieving the pressure of grades. A cumulative record is a good tool for diagnosing patterns of surface errors. A portfolio is a good tool for showing growth in writing. And on it goes.

So far this all sounds like common sense, right? But I have arrived at this toolbox metaphor after twenty years of abandoning old "wrong" grading techniques and adopting new "right" techniques. (I've done this a dozen times, perhaps.) Looking back on those abandoned techniques—the first ones and then the next ones and the later ones—I see that all of them had strong points. By the same token, all of them had weak points as well. The context made the difference!

However, as a profession, it seems to me that we are moving farther away from acknowledging context in instruction rather than closer to it. In fact, in recent years we have begun to ignore context and have adopted political (and sometimes religious) metaphors for particular instructional strategies (my grading options). [See the September, 1992, issue of *Language Arts* (NCTE). It is titled "Politics and Literacy."] I sometimes hear my colleagues referring to one teacher we know as "right-wing" because she does direct instruction of grammar. Another teacher I know has been called "leftist" because he grades his students' papers holistically. Whole language proponents are sometimes called "missionaries." Many of the teachers I know have begun to label one another, using these religious and political metaphors. (These same teachers fight heroically to avoid labeling students.) And sometimes the labels have led to antagonism. ("I can't believe she's so conservative that she's still teaching spelling! I thought she knew about the writing process. I just don't even feel like I can get through to her.")

Somehow we have created an implicit continuum for teaching and grading strategies. As best as I can construct it from the innuendos that surround it, it looks something like this:

"Liberal"	"Conservative"
holistic scoring	analytic scoring
student-centered approach	teacher-centered approach
peer response	teacher response
portfolios	grade-averaging
portfolios	cumulative records

(Grading strategies like primary-trait scoring, rubrics, teacher/student partnerships, and contracts are viewed as falling somewhere in the middle of this political continuum—they are "middle-of-the-road.")

But as I wrote the text for this book I kept constantly vigilant to avoid politically-charged categorizations like the one above. I believe that the political metaphor has left us in the position of sometimes throwing out, if not the baby with the bathwater, at least a perfectly good bar of soap. And so I argue for my toolbox metaphor. As teachers we need to analyze the communication context in which we find ourselves at any given moment in any given year and choose appropriately from among the many grading options that are open to us.

Chapter Summary

In order to choose among options and remain consistent to our teaching contexts, we must consider each corner of the communication triangle. Whether we begin with our own corner—the teacher corner—or whether we begin somewhere else, it is crucial that we take into account instructional purpose and student needs as well as our own point of view. At the same time, it is not helpful for us to label someone else (or ourselves) with a political label—"conservative" or "liberal"—based on evaluation (or, for that matter, teaching) choices. The important thing is to make sure our own choices are consistent with our teaching context.

EXERCISES

1. Design a grading system for the scenario that follows. Explain the choices you made.

   Scenario

   Mr. Lincoln teaches sixth grade in a big city school. Many of his students come from low-income families who speak a variety of "nonstandard" dialects of English. Some of his students want to go to college and are already focused on "doing well" in school. They perceive a need to learn "standard" English, and want to know the academic terms for what they are writing. Others are bored and wanting to quit school like their older brothers and sisters have done. Mr. Lincoln has been teaching for five years in this school, and he has a good grasp of the situation. He wants to support the students who want to concentrate on their academics, but he also wants to change the attitudes of some of the other students. Grades motivate the academically oriented students but threaten the others.

2. Write your own scenario, including information about the teacher, the students, and the instructional purposes. Design a grading system to fit your scenario. Write a letter to the parents of your students explaining what you will be doing and why.

3. In your mind, superimpose politics onto the scenarios presented in this chapter. Imagine that Mr. Jaramillio, Ms. Paxton, and Mrs. Begay all teach in the same school district. What political attacks might Mr. Jaramillio and Ms. Paxton make on each other? What might Mrs. Begay say to them both? Write a skit of a polarized faculty meeting using these characters. Share your skit with the other members of your group.

4. State your own ideas about how you wish to grade. Defend your ideas in nonaccusatory language without making reference to the shortcomings of other systems of grading.

References   *Language Arts*, September, 1992.

CHAPTER 10

Transcending the Red Ink
or Making Grading Serve Teaching

Making Grading Serve Teaching

When I first approached a publisher with the idea for this book, I was asked, "But why don't you write a book about *teaching* writing?"

My spoken answer was "Because that book has already been written, and written very well—several times." (See, for example, Gail Tompkins's book *Teaching Writing: Balancing Process and Product,* published by Merrill Publishing Company in 1990.) But my unspoken answer was "This book *is* about teaching writing."

One of the corners of the communication triangle as I have applied it to grading is "instructional purpose"—the teaching objective of the writing assignment. Throughout this book, in as many ways as I can think of, I have said, "Think about what you're trying to teach and evaluate on that. Make your evaluation serve your instruction."

This is harder than it sounds. How many times have I sat in the back of a classroom and watched an enthusiastic student teacher direct a fun writing activity that was so out of context that it had become meaningless? The student teacher had developed a lesson plan, but had no idea why a particular activity was being used, beyond the fact that the kids would like it. There was no instructional intentionality driving the lesson. Just as later no intentionality drove the evaluation of the piece of writing the students handed in (the product of the assignment).

And so this book is about teaching writing. It is about assessing student need, drawing on teacher expertise, identifying appropriate instructional objectives, and then choosing a grading tool that supports the teaching purpose of the writing assignment.

For the most part, communication-based grading is a matter of objectives and options, but now we come to the three *rules* of this kind of grading:

1. Analyze your grading/communication context and choose your evaluation tools when you *design* the writing assignment.
2. Tell your students how you will grade their papers *before* they begin to write.
3. Never grade on something you haven't taught.

When we are clear ourselves on where our students are, on what we think is important about writing, and on what we want to teach them to do next, we can make meaningful use of the fun writing activities that are as close as *Idea Exchange* (National Council of Teachers of English) and the teacher next door. But if we don't think ahead, or if we keep this information to ourselves and make our students guess at what it is we want them to learn from the activity, or if we refuse to teach them something because "they should have learned it last year" or "they're not ready for it," we cloud the issues monumentally.

Imagine for a moment an expert chef trying to teach a child to cook without first deciding on a recipe or teaching the child to use a measuring cup (or at least reviewing the process). Throughout the lesson the child would be anxious and guessing. "Are we making brownies?" "Or will we end up with oatmeal?" "I wish I could remember how much a teaspoon was!"

If the chef had not decided what they were trying to make, they might wind up with a concoction such as chocolate oatmeal or brownie mix with milk on it that no one would eat! And yet that is exactly what we do when we don't plan our criteria, tell our students ahead of time what our instructional goals are, and teach them what we expect them to know.

By deciding ourselves, telling our students what we plan to evaluate before they write, and teaching to our goals, we make evaluation serve an individual assignment. But how do we make evaluation serve our teaching of writing over the entire course of instruction? There are three techniques I have found useful for accomplishing this purpose: working with revisions of student writing, adding grading criteria over time, and progressive weighting of grades. Let's look at them one at a time.

Working with Revisions

If we look at writing and grading as processes, it makes sense to allow students to revise even after a piece has been evaluated. The grade is no more an end point than sharing or publishing is. If we are using grades to communicate, then it stands to reason that we want our students to respond to the communication: we want them to revise. And then we can revise the grade.

The only proviso I would make on student revisions is that they should be strictly voluntary. Sometimes a piece of writing is finished, whether it is "good" or not. And students know this best about their own work. If a student wishes to leave a piece as it is and go on to the next one, we should respect his or her wishes.

Adding Criteria over Time

The best way to reach any goal is to break the process of reaching that goal down into its component steps. If I want to write a book on evaluation, for example, I must first decide on my audience. Next I must sketch out an annotated map of the book I intend to write. Then I will approach a publisher. Next I will revise my ideas based on what the publisher knows about books. And so on, until I have finished my book. But if I say "I am going to write a book" and stop there, I will surely become paralyzed at the audacity of my thought!

The same is true for students. If we break down the process they must go through to move from where they are as writers to where we want them to be and then inform them of the steps one at a time, we keep them from the paralysis of the magnitude of the task before them. We grade first on one portion, then on a second, and so forth, until something has been learned. For example, Mr. Ashley, a fifth-grade teacher, begins the year by teaching the writing process. He evaluates the first two writing assignments solely on the process: evidence of prewriting, participation in peer revision groups, actual changes between drafts, and participation in the author's chair (class sharing of writing). Next he adds context. He teaches audience, purpose, and writer's stance. He evaluates assignments two and three on process and on context— the appropriateness of subject matter and language for a chosen audience, the accomplishment of the purpose of the writing, and the writer's voice. Next he adds structure. The class writes expository papers. He grades them on process, context, and structure. And so on until the end of the year Mr. Ashley is grading his students on a list of specified criteria.

Progressive Weighting of Grades

A third way to make evaluation serve instruction over time is to weight grades differently. As teachers we want growth, progress, in our student's work. Why then is the first piece of writing they do weighted as heavily as the last? Why not make the first few pieces worth three points, the next few five, and the last ten? This technique allows students time to write and develop as writers with increasing pressure to keep pace with increasing skill.

Beyond Evaluation: Alternative Purposes of Grading

Grading can be a useful tool beyond even its instructional purposes. It can give us important information about instructional design and teaching success. As we map out a long-term plan of evaluation goals, we are actually mapping out long-term instructional goals. And if we are certain that we have taught to our goals, we have followed our plan. This system of planning, teaching, and rechecking serves the same purpose as does course design. If I ask myself "What do I want to grade primary writers on?", I have asked myself "What do second-graders need to learn about writing this year?"

By the same token, thoughtful reflection at the end of the year about how well my students have met my evaluation criteria provides feedback about instructional success. If I have planned to teach (and evaluate) audience awareness with my third-graders and they are successful at writing differently to a class speaker and to the kindergartners down the hall, then my instruction has been successful. But if they do not alter vocabulary and topics to the different audiences—if, in fact, the majority of the class is getting low grades on audience awareness—my instruction needs improvement.

With this orientation toward the larger communication that grades can provide to us about our own work, grading becomes not only student-evaluation, but self-evaluation as well. Too many low grades among our students, then, result in a low mark for our instruction as well.

Questions of Power

How early do grades become synonymous with success and failure? How soon do they cause our stomachs to churn? Too early. The week before my daughter was to begin kindergarten, she told me with deep anxiety that she was afraid she was going to "flunk" because she couldn't yet hop on one foot in a straight line. (I have no idea where she got the information about hopping on one foot or about flunking; certainly I had never discussed either with her.) Last night (she is now a fifth-grader), after she finished decorating the folder her Halloween story was going into, she looked up at me and said wistfully, "I hope I get a good grade on my story." She did not say, "I'm proud of this story" or "I had fun working on this story" or even "I worked hard on this story and did what the teacher asked. I know I'm going to get a good grade." She said "I hope" in the same tone I use when it's been raining for a week and I say, "I hope the sun will come out this afternoon." And yet she did have fun working on the story and she had done a good job. So why the wistful tone?

Too often grades do cause kids to feel wistful (or angry, or frightened, or ashamed). In an ideal world where every child (or even most of them) came to school with an internalized self-esteem that had no reference to success or failure in school, grades would not have this power. But in the world in which we teach, grades have very great power, and no discussion of evaluation would be complete without some mention of that power. As graders, then, we hold great power over our students. We have all experienced teachers who have used that power for their own ends rather than for instructional ends (and perhaps sometimes we too have been guilty). And so I say that evaluation should be a tool made to serve instruction. It is not an end in itself; it is a means to an end.

How to keep the tool in its place? How to make it serve the teacher and the students rather than the other way around?

First, focus the grade on the writing product, not on the student. Say, "This is a great paper!" not "You did a great job." Jane may have done a great job in simply turning something in. Don's paper, on the other hand, may have been written by his grandmother. Assess the work, not the kid. If Jane's paper is not so great, she probably knows it, and she probably knows why. It is important to affirm for her that the paper needs more work. But it is not O.K. to say, "You're a better writer than this Jane—I expect better work from you." By the same token, Don knows if he didn't write his paper, whether the teacher ever finds out or not. By praising the paper (his grandmother, after all, did a lot of work on it!) but not him, the evaluation—and Don—are kept at least minimally honest.

But Jane and Don are extreme cases. Kids who have done their own work and done it to the best of their ability deserve an honest appraisal of the work. The teacher's opinion of their ability level is only that—an opinion. And mistaken opinions about abilities cause untold heartache.

After an in-service I recently conducted, an anxious teacher came up to me. He was middle-aged and very intense. "You know," he said, "I've always worked hard at my grading. I think it's so important for kids to be good writers. When I was in elementary school I was labeled learning disabled because I couldn't spell. I've spent the better part of thirty years overcoming that label. I don't want my students to experience what I did."

We all know stories like this one. In the last few years we've made a conscious effort to mainstream kids who are different to avoid labeling them one thing or another. But sometimes we forget that grades are labels too. How many times have you heard someone say to you, "I was a 'C'-student in school"? How different would it be if that same person said, "I wrote several 'C' papers in school." So label the work, not the kid!

But there is a second power concern. Earlier in this chapter I argued for telling students ahead of time what we want them to learn from a particular writing assignment and then evaluating them on only those announced goals. This procedure, which looks so simple at first glance, is really a power issue. When we keep our grading criteria to ourselves (or even worse—when we fail to articulate them, even to ourselves) we corner the power market for ourselves (or for our subconscious!). If our students are working to guess at what is important to us, they are focused on us rather than on their work. But when we share the goals, perhaps even formulating the goals in a partnership, we share the power of the grade as well. It is one thing if Maria knows clearly what the criteria for a particular writing assignment are and yet fails to meet them. It is something entirely different if she fails to meet criteria she knows nothing about. In the first case, if her grade is lower than she would like, she knows why and has a route open to her to correct the situation, a route that is much clearer than "I just have to work harder."

And, of course, there are the power issues related to the other adults in our students' lives. A third-grade teacher I know told me about a student in her class whose parents grounded him every time he brought home a grade lower than an "A." Principals have been known to place students (or refuse to place them) in enrichment programs of various titles (gifted, talented, etc.) based on a pattern of grades. Counselors have been known to refer students to special programs of all types based on grades. Beyond doing our best to educate people around us about what we are trying to communicate with our grades, there is very little we can do to change some of these larger issues. But, we must always take grades seriously. Often they have more power than we intend for them.

A World without Grades

In my ideal educational world, grading would not exist at all. (Lots of other things would be different too, but they are beyond the scope of this book.) Some progressive schools are attempting alternative approaches to evaluation. For example, I know of a district in which students are not given grades at all until they reach the fourth grade. I know of another school that is developing a system of portfolios of student work accompanied only by anecdotal records. But most of the schools I work in use grades and require teachers to provide grades to parents and students at regular intervals (sometimes every week, sometimes every nine weeks). To the teachers who are fortunate enough to work in environments without grades I say, "Bravo, and may your tribe increase!" But the rest of us are still faced with the realities of grades and power and politics. While we work toward a better educational system, it becomes important to find ways of transcending the sea of red ink we sometimes find ourselves awash in so that we can use evaluation to communicate about instruction with our students.

Chapter Summary

Sometimes we feel ourselves awash in a sea of red ink. Some schools are experimenting with systems without grades, but for most of us there is not yet any escape from grades. Therefore, we must make sure our evaluation is not separate from our instruction: we must make our evaluation serve our teaching.

EXERCISES

1. Design a year's evaluation plan to go with the beginning you made in Chapter 9, exercise 2. Explain how you could use evaluation to support the development of instructional purposes.

2. Explain how you could use the grading plan you designed in Exercise 1 to evaluate your own teaching for the year and revise your teaching for the following year.

CHAPTER 11

Teach Yourself to Grade
or the Grading Process in Action

Learning the Grading Process

Grading is a craft, just as calligraphy is a craft. To do calligraphy we must learn about oddly shaped pens, india ink, and textures of papers. We must study and practice the shapes of the alphabet, maybe even attempting gold illumination of tall letters on crackling onionskin.

But calligraphy can be an art as well. An artist-calligrapher who lived in my town died recently. As a coincidence, there happened to be a show of his work at the university art museum at the same time. (The show became a tribute show.) As I wandered up and down the rows, I was filled with excitement. This man (Dick Beasley was his name) had succeeded in making art from calligraphy. I had never seen calligraphy art before—pictures of energy, pictures of thanksgiving, pictures of ancient elegance—all made from the alphabet. The walls of the exhibit were punctuated with quotations from Dick about his work. One quotation spoke to the tension he felt between art and craft:

> The process, or medium, for me, is simply a means to an end, not an end in itself. The end product must stimulate visually my own eyes quite apart from the means I employ to execute the image. I claim no mastery over any process, but expect of myself enough technical competence not to be apologetic for the quality of any work produced by my own hands and mind. Art and craft, you realize, can in no way be separate from each other. Art is the concept, or mental image of the artist, craft is the making of that concept or image. This applies to any process or medium where an artist is imposing ideas upon materials for a given end.

Dr. Beasley's work displayed in the room included abstract designs, weavings, pottery, illuminated lettering, even certificates. All of the pieces testified to the fact that he had managed to take the stylized letters of his craft and make them his own, draw them so that they spoke what he, Dick Beasley, felt inside his soul. He had made his craft into an art.

And so it is with evaluation. To grade students' papers competently, we must learn what options we have and how to choose from among them. To grade them humanely and touch the art of teaching with our evaluation, we must become sensitive to the nuances in our instructional situations. To become the best teachers of students, we must adapt the tools to make them our own, to make them serve our instructional purposes.

But this is a how-to book. How, then, to . . . ?

First, no one but you can teach yourself to grade. A book or a workshop or a presenter can give you ideas, hints, and suggestions, but you must be in charge of your own learning. The learning of a craft or an art is as individual as every person who has ever become an artist or a craftsman. Usually, however, we learn crafts and arts by some combination of observation, learning of principles, and practice. As students ourselves we have had years of observing certain kinds of evaluation. As with any observation, however, our personal record is spotty, incomplete. The purpose of this book is to lay out the principles of evaluation—grading options. Grading cannot be learned from reading a book anymore than calligraphy can be learned from a book. The real learning takes place once the beginning artist or beginning grader begins to experiment and practice.

The writing process itself can point the way: Prewriting—Drafting—Rewriting—Sharing. Or is it Prewriting—Rewriting—Prewriting—Drafting—Sharing—Drafting—Rewriting—Sharing—Prewriting?

But then, like the writing process, perhaps the grading process can be untangled into primary activities: Pregrading—Guessing—Regrading—Grading. To me, "pregrading" means studying the communication situation and matching our options—this entire book, in fact; "guessing" means the first tentative grade we put on the first student papers; "regrading" means going back and making sure the grades we gave the first and last papers agree; "grading" means the moment when we commit ourselves and hand back the papers or send home the report cards. And maybe the grading process is just as recursive. Maybe it looks like the schematics of the writing process we have begun to draw, messy and recursive, bending back infinitely on itself until we finally just stop. In his book *Write to Learn*, Donald Murray offers a model of the writing process that illustrates the messy, recursive nature of writing, the jumble that happens in our heads (p. 6). His model is presented in Figure 11.1. Perhaps a graphic of the grading process (see Figure 11.2) would look much the same.

And as with writing, experimenting with grading is O.K.; in fact, it is mandatory if we are to truly match our evaluation to our instruction, if we are to

FIGURE 11.1. The Writing Process

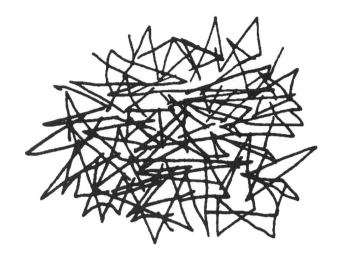

FIGURE 11.2. The Grading Process

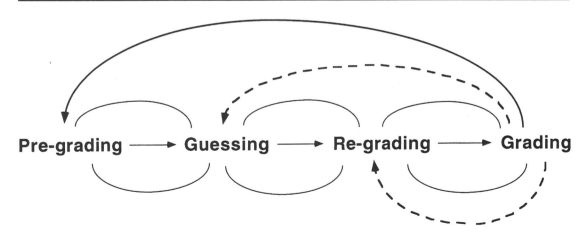

develop the individual grading system each of us as "teacher" needs, and if we are to find our own voices as graders.

In recent years I have had the pleasure of getting to know several fiction writers on a personal basis. One of the questions I love to ask is, "How do you write?" The answers are fascinating and varied. One writer I know writes in longhand on a yellow legal pad in the library. Another writer I know writes on a word processor in a study at home. In her book *The Writing Life,* Annie Dillard tells about a writer who does errands and then rushes into his house to retype everything he's written up to that point and add a sentence or two. Another writer I know of needs solitude so intensely that she moves to a new city whenever she is beginning a new book. Some writers drink, some listen to music, some eat popcorn. Oddly, perhaps, all of these writers are good writers. But how did these people develop these systems for writing? The answer is of course by writing, by practicing, by seeing what fit their personal work styles and what did not. Learning to grade is much the same.

Ways of Beginning

But lest I leave you where my teachers left me—"you have to work it out yourself"—I will lay out for you three scenarios of possible ways to begin teaching yourself to grade. Please remember, though, that these are only three of an almost infinite number of scenarios. If none of these works for you, strike out across the desert on your own. Do errands madly and then rush into your house to grade a paper or two.

Scenario #1

Begin from an analytic base. Find your district's (or state's) curriculum guide. Make a list of all of the writing skills someone else has compiled that are labeled as "appropriate" for the grade level you teach. Divide them into the five categories I have suggested in Chapter 3 (context, content, structure, mechanics, process). Read the paper once for context and content, a second time for structure, a third time for mechanics. Examine the process the student used. Pick up another student's work. Read that student's work in the same way as you did the first one's. Do this a hundred times or until the pieces begin to blur before your eyes and you can move toward primary-trait scoring and, finally, holistic scoring.

Scenario #2

Begin from a holistic base. Read a set of papers straight through. Without thinking too much, sort them into three piles—"Good," "O.K.," "Weak." Read your "Good" stack a second time and divide it into "Excellent" and "Good" and "Not Quite as Good as I Thought." Read your "O.K." stack a second time and divide it into "Pretty Good Really," "O.K.," and "Just Barely O.K." Read your "Weak" stack a second time and divide it into "Almost O.K.," "Weak," and "Needs Another Try." Sift through your stacks (you'll remember the papers this time) and double check that you've been fair. Move a paper or two around. If in doubt, move the paper to a higher stack (both you and the student will feel better and no harm will be done). Collapse your stacks ("Excellent" is stack one. "Good," "Not Quite as Good as I Thought," and "Pretty Good Really" is stack two. "O.K.," "Just Barely O.K.," and "Almost O.K." become stack three. "Weak" is a fourth stack.) Put grades on your stacks ("A" for stack one, "B" for stack two, "C" for stack three, "D" for stack four—or use the "+," "✓+," "✓," "✓−"). Give back the "Needs Another Try" stack, have conferences with those students, and ask them to re-do the assignment.

Do cluster grading a hundred times or until the stacks begin to have specific characteristics for you. Write down those characteristics. Make a rubric from your lists. Grade from your rubric until you are ready to examine the state's curriculum guide for more characteristics.

Scenario #3

Begin from a primary-trait base. If the pieces of the grading puzzle are new concepts for you, teach yourself to grade as you teach your students to write. You may begin with any piece of the puzzle you choose (I would recommend beginning with process). Using your state curriculum guide or the list in Chapter 3, make yourself a rubric that covers only that piece of the puzzle (the writing process—prewriting, drafting, revising, editing, publishing). Teach process to your students. Grade their papers only on process.

Now move to another piece of the puzzle—context perhaps. Make yourself a rubric about audience, purpose, and author's stance. Teach context concerns to your students. Evaluate their papers on process and context. Move to content, and so on. (A hint: if reading for mechanics is a problem, read the paper backwards, sentence by sentence. This exercise breaks up the meaning and allows you to examine the mechanics of the prose, sentence by sentence, almost as if it were a worksheet.)

Do this a hundred times or until you begin to get a feel for the pieces and for the whole. Try cluster grading. Try criterion-referenced grading.

Creating a Personal Grading System

Why teach yourself to grade using all the different approaches? You don't have to, of course. No one is going to come to your classroom with a five-year checklist and see if you've tried all of the approaches. But no grading strategy tells the whole story. Writing is an exceedingly complex behavior, and the different approaches to evaluating it offer us different bits of information about the process of becoming an articulate writer. From holistic grading we learn that writing is more than the sum of its parts. We acknowledge that a piece of writing can be heavily flawed (like Flannery O'Connor's drafts) and still be powerful and wonderful. We also acknowledge that writing can be flawless in design and still say absolutely nothing worth saying (a high school senior's five-paragraph essay on "the future"). From analytic grading we learn that writing can be taught, that we can oftentimes define for a writer what it is that he or she needs to work on to improve. I believe that it is important for any teacher who grades writing to understand all the approaches to grading. Only then can meaningful choices be made that match grading strategies to instructional goals.

Learning to grade is like learning any other craft. It is not easy to learn to grade, just as it is not easy to learn to ride a bicycle, fly an airplane, crochet an afghan, or create art from calligraphy. It takes a long time and a lot of practice to get good at evaluation. But because most of us teach ten, twenty, or even forty years, an investment of two or three years teaching ourselves to grade writing will pay off in the long run. The more intentional each of us becomes about evaluation, the more we each pick a system and practice with it, the quicker and more consistent we become. After several years of teaching and grading writing you may find that you grade very differently from the teacher next door. And guess what? That's O.K.

We teach and grade from our values. All of us value different things about different kinds of writing. (My husband likes to read travelogues that offer philosophical comments along the trail; I enjoy murder mysteries about characters who fool the world but not the detective.) As long as students understand clearly what we value about writing—what it is that we are trying to teach them—and as long as our evaluation reflects our instruction, our grades are "fair." Students stay in school for twelve to sixteen to twenty-two years. They have different teachers who teach them different things about writing. Thank goodness, right? So clarify for yourself what you value most about writing, match your instructional goals to those values, match your grading system to those instructional goals, inform your students of your system, and grade their papers with conviction!

Chapter Summary

Learning to grade involves both art and craft. The craft is knowing which tools to use in which situation. The art is in knowing what you want your grades to do. While learning to grade it is important to understand both analytic and holistic grading, so it is unimportant where on the continuum a teacher begins to learn to grade.

EXERCISES

1. Decide where on the grading approach continuum you want to begin learning to grade. Grade five papers from the Appendix according to the approach you have chosen.

2. Find someone in your group who began at a different point on the continuum. Swap papers (with the grades kept secret from each other). Grade the other teacher's papers using your approach. Ask the other teacher to grade yours using his or her approach. Compare the grades of all ten papers. Discuss any grades that are radically different. Is the difference a result of the method, or of your values as teachers, or of something else?

References   Beasley, Richard. Tribute Show. Flagstaff, AZ: Northern Arizona University Art Gallery, October–November, 1992.

Dillard, Annie. *The Writing Life*. New York: Harper and Row, 1990.

Murray, Donald. *Write to Learn*, 2nd ed. New York: Holt, Rinehart and Winston, 1987.

APPENDIX A
Sample Papers

Appendix A contains 30 samples of writing done by children in first through sixth grades. Wherever I could gather more than one sample from an assignment, I did so, attempting to provide samples that illustrated the range of work turned in to the teacher for evaluation. The samples illustrate a variety of instructional purpose and student audience, drawn as they were from different classrooms in schools sometimes over 100 miles apart. I have intentionally omitted the original context of the piece of writing: invent your own contexts for it. In the context of a primary classroom, Figure A.14 (for example) may represent excellent work; however, in the context of a sixth-grade classroom, it may represent work that needs to be done over. Experiment with instructional purpose as well. See what happens to the grade on the piece as the context changes. Trade papers with another teacher and see what happens to the grade. Discuss what you each did and why.

But beyond providing practice for grading and points of departure for discussion, this appendix illustrates the range and richness of children's writing. So use your own imagination, and enjoy the imaginations of the kids who so kindly allowed me to use their work.

FIGURE A.1. Fortunately/Unfortunately

FIGURE A.1. Fortunately/Unfortunately (continued)

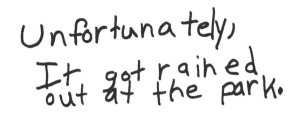

FIGURE A.1. Fortunately/Unfortunately (continued)

FIGURE A.1. Fortunately/Unfortunately (continued)

Unfortunately,
My house was a
mess.

FIGURE A.1. Fortunately/Unfortunately (continued)

Fortunately,
I had enough room to
fit the presents in and
I got
so. a SuperSoaker

FIGURE A.1. Fortunately/Unfortunately (continued)

Unfortunately, It got ran over by a car.

FIGURE A.2. Unfortunately/Fortunately

Fortunately my mom was going to buy me a monkey!

FIGURE A.2. Unfortunately/Fortunately (continued)

UnFortunately my mom didn't have enough money excpt for a dollar.

FIGURE A.2. Unfortunately/Fortunately (continued)

Fortunately we won the lottery

FIGURE A.2. Unfortunately/Fortunately (continued)

Unfortunately we couldn't find a place where people buy monkeys.

FIGURE A.2. Unfortunately/Fortunately (continued)

Fortunately we went to the Zoo and the zookeeper said that we could keep his monkey.

FIGURE A.2. Unfortunately/Fortunately (continued)

Unfortunately it was not house trained.

FIGURE A.2. Unfortunately/Fortunately (continued)

Fortunately we trained her
we named her Lily.

FIGURE A.3. Spring Break

<u>Spring Break</u>

He came from the earth, a great mass of writhing darkness, darker than the blackest night. The master of darkness, the world from which he came knew no light. Great sharp talons that reached out, long and bony, were it's only real features and he came to destroy them, to catch them sleeping safe and sound in their warm little beds and do away with them all.

The smoke rose in dark puffs, visible against the pale winter sky. Inside the cottage, the awful stench of rot and decay was strong. The children's cheeks were hollow with hunger and the mother sat silently staring into the fire from her chair. The harsh winter winds blew fiercely outside, shaking the small shack and making the bare, finger like branches of the trees dance wildly about. To add to all of that, there came a strange mournful wail that threaded it's way through the forest and came dwindling to mere wisps at the door. Everyone was aware of it. The smallest children shuddered violently against the fierce cold and the eerie sound. The older children tried to ignore the steadily growing moan but soon they too were gathered around their mother, all eyes begging for reassurance and comfort. The mother did her best to dry their tears and build up the dying fire but she could not offer an explanation for this strange and frightening noise. Just as the sound was beginning to grow beyond bearing, everything stood still, the wind stopped and the moaning sound ceased to surround them.

The silence was like an explosion, it seemed to enclose them in an envelope of darkness and in that awful stillness, a blood curdling scream split the air and the dying fire sputtered and went out. The family stood frozen until the piercing sound of another scream aroused them into an intense terror that none had ever known before. It was so strong that everyone seemed to be out of breath from the weight of it. Then the rumbling sound began, It was similar to the sound of distant thunder rolling gently along the hills but at the same time, the earth began to shake, gently at first but then violently, sending everyone and everything shattering to the floor.

The children screamed, terrified, as the ground beneath them heaved upward and then began to tilt. There were several deffening explosions that sent earth, rock, tree and many splintered cottages tumbling through the air. Cries for help from other women and children could be heard everywhere and with the last lights of day disappearing over the horizon, the night set in. No moon rose and no twinkling starlight gave even the slightest hint of light and in the utter blackness, raging fires could be seen burning like brilliant flowers in a land of rubble and dust. The strong voice of a man cut through the darkness like a ray of light, "Do not despair," he said and paused. Many cries of protest went up and he went on, "Do you remember the legend of the underworld and how it's king would one day rise up and take our land, destroying us? This legend has been passed down for many generations and now, this very second he sets forth from the

144 APPENDIX A *Sample Papers*

FIGURE A.3. Spring Break (continued)

place where he erupted from the earth to conquer us. The strange
sounds you just heard were the sounds of the earth and the trees
and all living things announcing his coming. All the men of this
village and many others have gone to meet this evil creature they
call king of the underworld and hold him back until more help is
sent." Who shall protect us?" a weak voice cried out from
somewhere in the darkness.

"All the men from this land will come together to fight this
evil creature. Until it has been destroyed you will have to fend
for yourselves, I am sorry." His voice was strained and sad as he
said these last words as if it hurt him to say them. Then he was
gone and the people of the village began picking through the
wreck of smashed houses and gathering together for warmth. In the
morning it was still pitch black and throughout all that day and
the next the sun did not shine and no word came from the north
where the great battle was being fought. Sometimes small groups
of men carrying pitchforks and torches could be seen marching
northward. At first these men were always cheered on by the women
and children but after a while everyone was so tired and weak
that they could barely speak to each other without collapsing
with the effort. Sometimes they gathered around in a circle and
told what little they could remember from the legend of the
underworld.

Seven days passed in complete darkness and on the seventh
night the stars shone bright in the sky and a beautiful moon rose
full over the troubled land. At dawn the sky grew pink and the
sun rose with a blinding fierceness. Along with the restoring of
the sun there came a runner from the north bearing a message. He
reported that the battle had been fought and won by the villagers
and that the king of the underworld had been killed and flung off
the edge of the world, never to haunt the land again. The men of
the village were cleaning up the mess and working their way back
toward the home.

With this relieving news, the women and children were filled
with a surprising new strength and began to clean up the awful
wreck in the village. By the time the mess had been totally
cleared away and the men came marching over the hill and down
into the valley there was much celebrating and feasting that
lasted far into the warm days of spring, Spring brought a promise
of a new beginning. The trees that had slept for so long during
those dark winter months awakened with a joyful explosion of
delicate green leaves. The grass grew soft where nothing but
crunching leaves had blown silently across barren ground and the
crops grew plentifully. No one was hungry and everyone was in
good health.

They lived in peace forever and always remembered the seven
days of darkness in which the great battle was fought. In fact
they decided to take a seven day vacation from work and school in
memory of those seven days of darkness and the people that fought
through them. This vacation is now commonly refered to as spring
break and not a single person remembers the reason we have it.

FIGURE A.4. Dear Penny . . .

Dear Penny,
     I think it would be
hard to train a gorilla. I have
always wanted a gorilla like Koko.
I wont to know is it fun playing
with Koko?

               Your friend,
               Miriam

FIGURE A.5. The Anasazis

WHY THE ANASAZI'S DISAPPEARED?

One hot summer night, in a beautiful desert place named Red Canyon, some Indians were sitting around a fire telling stories about how the white men came and took their land and killed their people. All of a sudden they heard some sticks crackling behind them in the bushes. One of the Indians grabbed his bow and arrow and said to the noise in the bushes, "Come out of there and show your face to us Indians." Then a white man stepped out from behind the bushes. The Indian said, "Get off my land!" The white man said, "No, this is not your land this land is the governments land." "You barbarians are ruining the land." "And those marking (petroglyphs) you wrote all over the mountains, what do they mean?" The Indian said. "Those are our special prayers." "We do not want you white men carving your names and dates all over them and ruining our messages." "Now leave our land before you ruin anything else." Then the Indian pointed his bow and arrow at the white man and said, "Go and leave me and my people alone." The white man said, "Okay, I will leave, but I will be back for you and your people."

After the white man left, one of the Indian kids said, "What will happen to us when the white men come back?" The Indian man said, "We won't be here when the white men come back for us." Everyone said, "What do you mean we won't be here when the white men come back?" The Indian man said, "We are going to move to a new home." So all of the Indians packed their things and left. The next day a whole army of white men came to the Indian village. they looked all over but couldn't find the Indians. And to this day no one knows what happened to those Indian people.

FIGURE A.6. China

I know three
things about China
They use Chopstiks
To eat They bilt a
grato wol to Keep the
enomes out uv ther
viligs They eat rise.

FIGURE A.7. My mom is . . .

my mom is realea helips us bekus she iis a mirse, well she yustoo be but now she isa nursing assistant teacher. I Love her. She reeds to me. She tux me in at nite. She is rile bise. She is a verel good cook. She pras with me She givs me mune if I do my work. She bis me toys and school ekwimint. And plas gams with me.

FIGURE A.8. A Ship

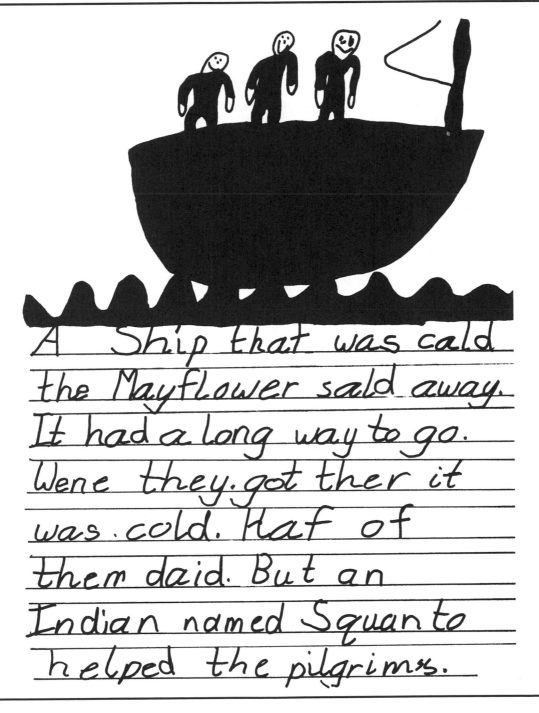

A Ship that was cald
the Mayflower sald away.
It had a long way to go.
Wene they got ther it
was cold. Haf of
them daid. But an
Indian named Squanto
helped the pilgrims.

FIGURE A.9. A Sequel to Tom Sawyer

(A sequel to a chapter from Tom Sawyer)

Tom was so sad after Becky had said those words to him. He felt sick again. Actually Becky liked him too, but didn't admit it. Tom went home sad as ever, so did Peter.

Aunt Polly said, "Tom, what's a matter with you? You look like your stomach fell out."

"Well," said Tom. "Becky Thatcher has been out of school for a long time and I missed her a lot. She just came back today and well, Aunt Polly, I'm tired, I'm gonna rest."

"OK Tom," answered Aunt Polly.

Tom thought and thought about what to say to Becky. Finally he said, "I'll just be me for awhile."

As they were eating supper, Aunt Polly thought about what was wrong with Tom.

Tom said, "What's a matter with Peter?"

"Why, I don't know, Tom," answered Aunt Polly.

"I was just wondering because he sleeps all the time." explained Tom.

What was wrong with Peter was that he liked Becky too. He went to his bed thinking about how in the world he could get Becky to like him. Tom didn't know that Peter liked Becky because he was too busy thinking about how to get to sleep. Finally both of them fell asleep.

When Tom woke he ate breakfast quickly and ran to school as fast as he could.

There was Becky standing in the schoolyard talking to her friends. Tom walked into the schoolyard whistling a happy tune.

Becky noticed and said, "There's Tom Sawyer, isn't he cute!" They all giggled. Little did Tom know that he was in for a big surprise.

After school Becky said to Tom, "My birthday party is tomorrow, could you come?"

Tom was so overjoyed that he said, "Yes, I can come!"

"Great," said Becky. "See you tomorrow."

"Bye," said Tom.

Tom ran home. He burst through the door and yelled, "Aunt Polly!"

"Yes, I'm in the kitchen," answered Aunt Polly. "What is it?"

"I'm going to Becky's birthday party tomorrow, ok?" asked Tom.

"That's fine Tom, but be careful," decided Aunt Polly.

"I will, I promise," said Tom.

The next morning Tom dressed himself in his Sunday best. "Bye, Aunt Polly," waved Tom.

"Bye Tom, have a good day at school," said Aunt Polly.

FIGURE A.9. A Sequel to Tom Sawyer (continued)

Tom had an excellent day at school. He got good grades on all of his tests. Then it came, it was time for Becky's birthday party. All the kids rushed to Becky's house.

They played games, and then it was time for cake and ice cream. Becky's mom gave the first piece to Becky, then some to Tom and the rest of the kids. Tom said, "This is a really fun birthday, I've had a really great time."

"Thanks," said Becky and she kissed him on the cheek.

Tom had finally won Becky's heart, but he still had not figured out what was wrong with Peter.

FIGURE A.10. Mr. Ed

Mr. Ed was at the laundromat at noontime. He was feeling angry and bad. He had lost his job at J.B.'s restaurant a few hours ago. He had been a waiter there.

Earlier in the morning he and his wife had gotten in an argument. His wife had shouted at him "Fine" and stormed out of the house. He tried to call her back, "Ellen, come back." But she didn't respond or turn around. So he went to work upset. He thought during lunch, "I'll bring some flowers and we'll have a great brunch. Everything will be fine." But as it turned out he was wrong. The customers accused him of shouting at them. Then shortly afterwards he was yelling at his boss. Mr. Hogan, his boss, said, "Don't bother coming over tomorrow for work, you're fired!"

So he got in his car and he drove to his wife's office. They both apologized to each other. But after he told her how he got fired, she again stormed out and went home. When he got home she had his clothes on the porch. She started screaming words that he never heard her say before. All of a sudden before he knew what was happening the door slammed. He was just about to get in his car when he heard her come out and say, "Don't come back!" Questions were running through his head. Where am I going to stay? How will I get food? What if I die! HELP me somebody.

Monkey Bars

Slippery, hard and cold
My hands go across the bars and cross back.
It makes my arms tired,
But I like it.

Béésh ndaaz' ahígíí

Bídéelto', ntɬiz, dóó sik'az
　　(

Shila' béésh ndaaz' ahígíí bee tsé'
　　naa aɬnáhaná shchaɬ dóó nat' áá
　　　　((

Shigaan ninadalna, ndi shiɬ yá á tééh.

FIGURE A.12. My Favorite Author

My Favorite Author: H.G. Wells

H.G. Wells was born in 1886. He was a great author in his time. He wrote "romantic fiction," which was what they called science-fiction at that time. He earned a scholarship to the Normal School of Science in London. He wrote science articles for some magazines. He then wrote THE TIME MACHINE, which many consider his most well-written work. The success of that book started a career in which he in his "great period" wrote THE ISLAND OF DR. MOREOU (1896), THE INVISIBLE MAN (1897), THE WAR OF THE WORLDS (1898), WHEN THE SLEEPER WAKES (1899) and THE FIRST MEN IN THE MOON (1901). He wrote these books about a century ago, and they are still popular today because he wrote so well. After the turn of the century, Wells began writing social issue books. When he became less successful, he started to write short stories; these had normal success.

My favorite book written by Wells is THE INVISIBLE MAN. It is about a man who found a way to become invisible. He found out that he didn't have an antidote. He wanted to use his invisibility to his advantage. He started a "reign of terror" in which those who did not obey his commands would be murdered. At the end, the people catch the invisible man.

Two interesting things happened with Wells' stories. Winston Churchill liked the story THE LAND IRONCLADS and later designed tanks after the ones of which Wells had written. Another thing that happened was that one Halloween night in the 30's a radio station was doing THE WAR OF THE WORLDS, which is about Martians taking over our world. It sounded so real to people who tuned in at the middle that they panicked, thinking that the Martians were really taking over the world.

I like Wells' books because they have good dialect and dialogue. I also like his characters. He always has a "bad guy" or "bad guys," but there really isn't a hero because everybody seems so dimwitted. The settings aren't very important in the books he wrote; the story is really interesting by itself, but the setting doesn't help you understand it more. I like his science-fiction ideas because they are things that everybody dreams about. He really likes to do that kind of thing. This is why I like his books.

FIGURE A.13. The Plane

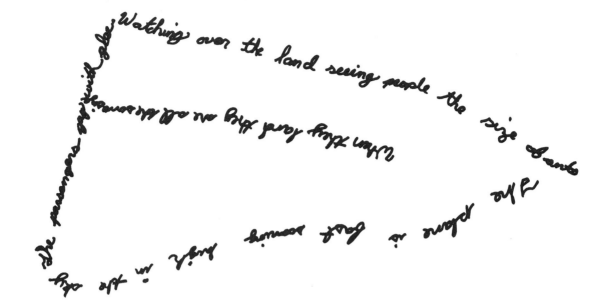

FIGURE A.14. The important thing about whales . . .

The important thing about whales is that they are almost gone. Killer whales are members of the dolphin family. Whales are nice. Whales are very big. Whales are mammals. Killer whales live in the cold waters. But the important thing about whales is that they are almost gone.

FIGURE A.15. The important thing about my dog . . .

The important thing about my dog is she is a Golden Retriever. She is special to my family. She is my best friend. She plays with me. She loves me. But the important thing about my dog is that she is a Golden Retriever.

FIGURE A.16. Stomach

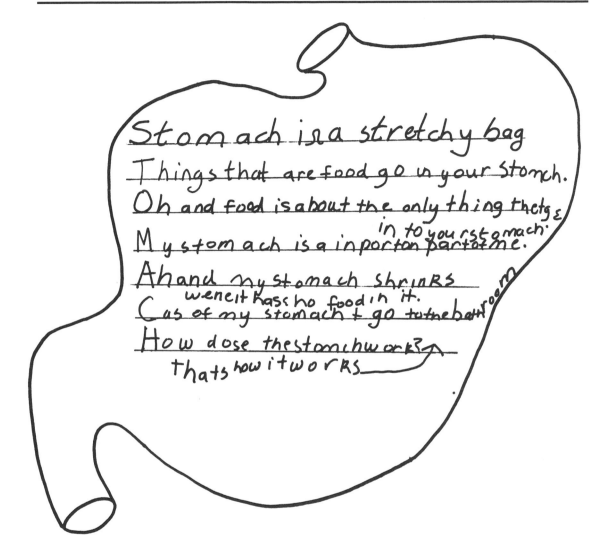

Stomach is a stretchy bag
Things that are food go in your Stomch.
Oh and food is about the only thing thetg
in to your rstomach.
My stomach is a inporton part of me.
Ahand my stomach shrinks
wene it hass no food in it.
Cas of my stomach t go tothebathroom
How dose thestomchwork?
thats how it works

FIGURE A.17. Muscles

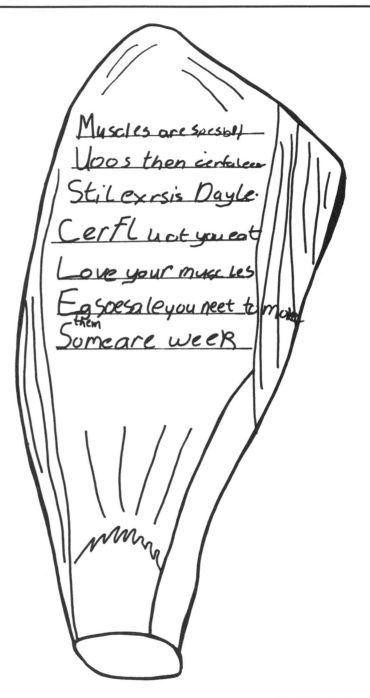

FIGURE A.18. Excited

SYNESTHETIC POETRY

Excited

LOOKS LIKE a scared cat

TASTES LIKE a juicy cherry

SMELLS LIKE cotton candy

SOUNDS LIKE yelling for joy

FEELS LIKE a rough stone

FIGURE A.19. Excited (second example)

SYNESTHETIC POETRY

excited

LOOKS LIKE Fire worchs

TASTES LIKE bubbles

SMELLS LIKE Fire

SOUNDS LIKE explosion

FEELS LIKE earthquake

FIGURE A.20. A Persian Kitten

A Persian Kitten

A Persian Kitten is white and fluffy, like a cloud

This Persian kitten plays with string, like a dog trying to catch a snake

Soon the kitten gets tired, but soon after her nap she will play agin.

This Pesian kitten likes to stay inside were it is warm and cosy.

This kitten will grow up and wan't be as playful but I will still rember when she

was a kitten.

FIGURE A.21. A Great Person

A Great Person

Born in 1706

He published a newspaper,

He was Philadeqia's Postmaster,

He was the father of the Govener of New Jersey,

He wrote the Almanac, and

He flew a kite. These are not all of the

wonderful things He did.

Do you know hoo this Person was?

This great person was... Bergaman Franklin.

FIGURE A.22. I like to play . . .

I like to play hideing go seek. This is how you play hideing go seek. It Li.e if someone is goingto count number and wine the other pirsin will triy to find you and if he or she find you have to cant if you find he or she and then she or he find you you just need to be doing the same thing I told you on the papen you gust nid to Polo the rols at I git you I pirsin Ride to cant in TaPyou can been

FIGURE A.23. How you play . . .

This How you play hockey
you get to get a hockey stick
. But there are rules
I do not fight. 2 do not hit.
that are all the rules.
Now you got to drop the puck
in the middle then you
hit the puck into the
goal if you make 20 ponits
you winner the game.

FIGURE A.24. Dear Matt . . .

Dear Matt,

Thank you for the letter I enjoyed reading it, you said you liked the Phoenix Suns I went to see them January 30th. They played Dallas Mavericks. The Suns won by 15 points.

I don't really care for football but I watch it occasionally and played in 1st grade. Have you played other sports?

I'm going to Lake Havasu this month. I've never been there before, is it a nice town.

Yes I do go cross contry skiing and I've been down hill once. My family goes skiing about once a weekend. You should come up here and try it some time. You'll probally like it. I have one brother named Joshua who is 4. I also have a ginea pig named Colorfull, a dog named Spot, four salamaders and a toad. Do you have any pets, brothers or sisters? Hope write you'll soon.

Sincerely,
Tom

FIGURE A.25. Dear William . . .

Dear William.
    I am 10 yeas old
also I would like to
know why your called
Brett when your name
is William?
    I was born in
flagstaff and lived in
the same house all my
live. I really don't
have a favorite pet
because I like them
all the same. My sister
is 7. How old is

FIGURE A.25. Dear William . . . (continued)

your brother?

How long have you lived in Lake Havasu? my Omi(grandma) just boeght a house there.

I used to play soccer in 1st and 2nd grade but it got boring.

I liked your letter please write back!

Sincerely

John

FIGURE A.26. The Beaver

___

THE BEAVER

THE BEAER

The beaver is a very diffrent and interesting animal. When beaver are born they are called kits, they weigh 8 to 24 ounces, are 15 inches long, and their tail is 3½ inches long. By their third summer ready to mate. A female beaver first breeds when its 2½ years old. The young stay with their mother till their second year. When the young are gone, the mother has another litter.

Beavers are builders, by cutting down trees with their teeth, they build dams, lodges, and canals. Some wood they sink in the water near their lodge (dam or canal). This will form an under-water storehouse, for keeping their winter food. Beavers live most of their life in or near water. Have you learned more about beavers than you use to know?

MY source is Comtons Encyclopedia

___

FIGURE A.27. Bald Eagles

Bald Eagles are intereresting birds. They are called the bald eagle because if you are far away they look bald. They lay ~~too~~ two eggs each year. The bald eagles have white on their heads. They eat fish and snatch it out of the water with there talons. They have big talons for big fish. The bald eagles build there nests to last for 12 months.

FIGURE A.28. Iguanas

IGUANAS

THE IGUANA IS A WEIRD SPECIE. THEY LIKE HOT PLACES. IF YOUR SHOULDER IS HOT AND THE IGUANA IS COLD IT WILL LAY ON YOUR SHOULDER. THEY LIKE TO EAT BANANAS, APPLES, AND ROMAIN LETTUCE. THEY LIVE IN THE DESERT. THEY LIVE 10 TO 12 YEARS IN CAPTIVITY.

IGUANAS ARE A COMMON REPTILE IN ARIZONA. THEY GROW TO BE 5 FEET LONG. THEY HAVE NO TEETH. THEY HAVE TWO ROUND BLACK MARDS AND THOSE ARE PRESENT IN THE IGUANAS CHEEKS.

SOURCE: ALL ABOUT IGUANAS
　　　　　BY MERVIN F. ROBERT AND
　　　　　MARTHA D. ROBERT

FIGURE A.29. My Earliest Memory

My Earliest Mememory

When I was about four ~~or~~ or five I went to the carnival with my brother, my stepdad. We also had a boy mambed Tom. We babysit him. His mom is my moms freind. We lived in the same hause we live in right know,

As lots of kids love to do I love to go on rides. You know, rides that are like at the festival in the pines or the carnival that they have once a year. When I get really dizzy I seem get kind of sick,

That day we went to the carnival that my family was really excited about. My parents play in a band, so they like to watch other bands so we watched the bard for a while. When ~~their~~ their was good songs Wayne and Tom and I were jumping up and down so excited because watching the band was getting kind of boring. Wayne and Tom and I wanted to go an more rides and play games. You know, the games that you throw the arrows and pop balloons. Finally mom let us go on rides. Wayne and I saw this ride we had to on It. It looked so fun. Then my mom let us go on it. When we got on, it went so fast it was great. Then it started going faster. I was practically turning blue. I felt like I was going to throw up. I was so sick. I felt like I. I remember that feeling really well. When the ride stopped Wayne and Tom wouldn't get off. They wanted to go again. Finally they got of, and my stepdad picked me up.

FIGURE A.30. My Earliest Memory (second example)

My Earliest Memory

When I was about three or four, I lived in Maine. I remember the house we lived almost perfectly. Well, I remember the outside perfectly. It was a white house with red shutters and a red back porch.

There were some kids across the street from us named Jaimie and Nicole. Jaimie was a boy, and Nicole was a girl. They were friends of ours. They were fun to play with too.

One day the older kids (which were my brother, Jaime and Nicole) decided go to a street called Garfield (Garfield Street was named after the president). I rode on the back of Nicole's bike. We went to a path in the trees that leads to Garfield Street.

As we were entering the path I screamed, I thought we were going to see Garfield the cat. And that's where my memory ends. Nothing more, nothing less.

APPENDIX B
Annotated Bibliography

Research and Theory

Ackerman, John. *Students' Self-Analysis and Judges' Perceptions: Where Do They Agree?* Technical Report #23. University of California, Berkeley: Center for the Study of Writing, May 1989.

> This study argues that giving and responding to a writing assignment is an act of negotiation that depends on at least seven variables. The writing task was divided into source, format, and plan; student perceptions and judges' perceptions of these categories were compared.

Anson, Chris M., ed. *Writing and Response: Theory, Practice, and Research.* Urbana, IL: National Council of Teachers of English, 1989.

> This collection of sixteen essays addresses a wide range of theoretical issues grouped into three large categories: toward a theory of response in the classroom community, new perspective for responding to writing, and studies of response in the instructional context.

Applebee, Arthur N., et al. *Learning to Write in Our Nation's Schools: Instruction and Achievement in 1988 at Grades 4, 8, and 12.* The National Assessment of Educational Progress, prepared by Educational Testing Service, June 1990.

> Of particular interest is the discrepancy between student perceptions and teacher perceptions of feedback on completed work (pp.53–56).

Cooper, Charles R. and Lee Odell, eds. *Evaluating Writing: Describing, Measuring, Judging.* Urbana, IL: National Council of Teachers of English, 1977.

> This collection of six essays summarizes methods of describing writing and measuring its growth. Essays cover holistic evaluation, primary-trait scoring, computer-aided description of mature word choices in writing, early blooming and late blooming syntactic structures, measuring changes in intellectual processes as one dimension of growth in writing, individualized goal setting, self-evaluation, and peer evaluation.

Dyson, Anne Haas and Sarah Warshauer Freedman. *On Teaching Writing: A Review of the Literature.* Occasional Paper #20. University of California, Berkeley, Center for the Study of Writing, July 1990.

> This bibliography is an invaluable tool for a survey of the literature. A section on the evaluation of writing (pp. 7–9) cites sources that discuss classroom issues, local issues, and national issues.

Freedman, Sarah Warshauer. *Evaluating Writing: Linking Large-Scale Testing and Classrom Assessment.* Occasional Paper #27. University of California, Berkeley, Center for the Study of Writing, May 1991.

> This paper focuses on large-scale testing and classroom assessment in an attempt to bridge the gap between teachers of writing and the testing and measurement community. A lengthy (and useful) reference list is appended.

Harmon, John. "The Myth of Measurable Improvement." *English Journal* 77 (9/1988): 79–80.

> This essay argues that because writing skill develops over a long period of time, a portfolio grading system makes the most sense.

Horvath, Brooke K. "The Components of Written Response: A Practical Synthesis of Current Views." In *The Writing Teacher's Sourcebook,* New York: Oxford University Press, 1988.

> This essay summarizes and synthesizes some of the guidelines, based on a study of the literature, for making effective written comments on student papers. The basic concern of the essay is with formative rather than summative evaluation.

Hyslop, Nancy B. "Evaluating Student Writing: Methods and Measurements," ERIC Clearinghouse on Reading and Communication Skills, March 1990.

> This page and a half digest synthesizes nine major contributions between 1977 and 1988 to the field of evaluating student writing.

Krest, Margie. "Time on My Hands: Handling the Paper Load." *English Journal* 76 (12/1987): 37–42.

> This essay redefines the role of "teacher" as it redefines the role of evaluation of student writing. It provides an overview of timesaving techniques as well.

Lees, Elaine O. "Evaluating Student Writing." In *The Writing Teacher's Sourcebook,* 2nd ed., edited by Gary Tate and Edward P. J. Corbett, pp. 263–267. New York: Oxford University Press, 1988.

> This essay looks at writing evaluation from a communication perspective: what do I as evaluator have to say to my student as an audience? The author discusses seven kinds of responding: correcting, emoting, describing, suggesting, questioning, reminding, and assigning.

Lindemann, Erika. *A Rhetoric for Writing Teachers.* New York: Oxford University Press, 1987.

> Chapter 13 of this book (pp. 191–223) is titled "Making and Evaluating Writing Assignments." In this chapter, the author discusses the relationship between grading and making writing assignments. She also discusses the various reasons for grading and some of the options available to teachers.

Schriver, Karen A. *Evaluating Text Quality: The Continuum from Text-Focused to Reader-Focused Methods.* Technical Report #41. University of California, Berkeley, Center for the Study of Writing, March 1990.

> This report focuses on methods available to writers for evaluating the effectiveness of the texts they produce. It begins by isolating persistent questions raised by

readers and then reviews typical methods of writer evaluation in three classes: text-focused, expert-judgment focused, and reader-focused approaches.

Shaugnessy, Mina. *Errors and Expectations: A Guide for the Teacher of Basic Writing.* New York: Oxford University Press, 1977.

While the population with which Shaugnessy worked was college freshmen, this book is a classic in the field of evaluation. Its basic premise is that student writing errors are not simply careless or random, that, in fact, they are consistent within the writing of any single student, and can be analyzed for patterns to determine what relearning must take place to achieve correct written language.

Sperling, Melanie. *I Want to Talk to Each of You: Collaboration and the Teacher-Student Writing Conference.* Technical Report #37. University of California, Berkeley, Center for the Study of Writing, October 1989.

This study examines interactive teacher-student writing conferences. Using ethnographic procedures, the study examines conferences over a six-week period for six case study ninth-graders.

Tiedt, Iris McClellan. *Writing: From Topic to Evaluation.* Boston: Allyn and Bacon, 1989.

This book contains explanations of contemporary theories about teaching writing and sample applications designed to illustrate how to put the theory into practice. Methods of evaluation that are discussed include analytic, holistic, and primary-trait. Self-evaluation and peer evaluation strategies are also included.

White, Edward M. "Post-structural Literary Criticism and the Response to Student Writing." In *The Writing Teacher's Sourcebook,* 2nd ed., edited by Gary Tate and Edward P. J. Corbett, pp. 285–293. New York: Oxford University Press, 1988.

In this essay, the author draws parallels between post-structuralist literary criticism and the practice of process-oriented writing teachers in reading and responding to student papers.

Classroom Practice

Belanoff, Pat and Marcia Dickson, eds. *Portfolios: Process and Product.* Portsmouth, NH: Boynton/Cook (Heinemann), 1991.

This collection of essays addresses questions of evaluation of portfolios in different contexts. Of particular interest are the essays collected in Section III—Classroom Portfolios, pp. 151–228.

Bunce-Crim, Mana. "New Tools for New Tasks." *Instructor* 101, 7 (March, 1992): 23–26.

This article offers tips and techniques for ongoing evaluation of primary and elementary age students. It details a system that includes observation, conferencing, and student self-assessment.

Cleary, Linda Miller. *From the Other Side of the Desk: Students Speak Out about Writing.* Portsmouth, NH: Boynton/Cook (Heinemann), 1991.

Of particular interest in this fascinating case-study book is the section entitled "Problems with Writing Curricula" (pp. 150–161). In addition, reflections on evaluation of writing are imbedded throughout the student stories.

Goodman, Kenneth, Yetta M. Goodman, and Wendy J. Hood, eds. *The Whole Language Evaluation Book.* Portsmouth, NH: Heinemann, 1989.

> The essays collected in this book center around particular stories of individual classrooms. The book is rich in student writing examples and evaluation forms created by teachers for various purposes.

Graves, Donald H. *Writing: Teachers and Children at Work.* Portsmouth, NH: Heinemann, 1983.

> Chapters 28 and 29, "Record Each Child's Development" and "Share the Children's Development with Parents and Administrators," give practical step-by-step directions for record keeping and communication. Eleven different kinds of records are discussed.

Haley-James, Shirley. "Twentieth-Century Perspectives on Writing in Grades One through Eight." In *Perspectives on Writing in Grades 1–8,* edited by Shirley Haley-James. Urbana, IL: National Council of Teachers of English, 1981.

> A portion of this essay (pp. 14–16) offers an interesting historical summary of methods of evaluation from 1900 to 1979.

Linck, Wayne M. "Grading and Evaluation Techniques for Whole Language Teachers." *Language Arts* 68, 2 (February, 1991): 125–132.

> This article explains three systems for grading: individual comparison techniques, group comparison techniques, and criteria comparison techniques.

Mayher, John S., Nancy Lester, and Gordon M. Pradl. *Learning to Write, Writing to Learn.* Portsmouth, NH: Boynton/Cook (Heinemann), 1983.

> Chapter 7 of this book, "Responding and Evaluating," offers examples of teacher response to reprinted student texts. Categories include teacher response, collaborative peer response, conferencing, and editing. Content-area writing is an added dimension of this text.

Moffett, James and Betty Jane Wagner. *Student-Centered Language Arts, K–12.* Portsmouth, NH: Boynton/Cook (Heinemann), 1992.

> Chapter 10, "Evaluation," discusses five functions of evaluation and offers strategies for inside-the-classroom evaluation as well as for outside-the-classroom evaluation. Classroom strategies include observation, charting, portfolios, and conferences.

Spandel, Vicki. *Classroom Applications of Writing Assessment: A Teacher's Handbook.* Clearinghouse for Applied Performance Testing, May 1981. In ERIC ED214995.

> This handbook was written to meet the needs of the classroom teacher who is teaching writing and who wishes to use performance-based assessment strategies: holistic, analytic, and primary-trait.

Spandel, Vicki and Richard Stiggins. *Creating Writers: Linking Assessment and Writing Instruction.* New York: Longman, 1990.

> Chapter 5, "Grading: What It Will and Will Not Do," discusses what grades are, what to grade, and when to grade. Special emphasis is given to analytical grading.

Tchudi, Stephen N. and Susan J. Tchudi. *The English/Language Arts Handbook.* Portsmouth, NH: Boynton/Cook (Heinemann), 1991.

> Chapter 4, "Assessment, Evaluation, and Grading," distinguishes between assessment, which describes and documents what is happening; evaluation, which imposes judgment standards on assessment; and grading, which condenses assessment and evaluation into a symbol.

Tompkins, Gail E. *Teaching Writing: Balancing Process and Product.* Columbus, OH: Merrill Publishing Co., 1990.

> Chapter 10, "Assessing Students' Writing," focuses on three types of assessment for elementary age students: informal monitoring, process assessment, and product assessment. Samples of questions to ask in conferences, checklists, anecdotal records, and self-assessment questionnaires are included. Communication with parents is also discussed.

Specific Strategies

Analytic Scoring

Stoneberg, Bert, Jr. "Analytic Trait Writing Assessment." A report of the Greater Albany Public Schools District Assessment of Writing of Students in Grades 5, 7, 9, and 11. Greater Albany, Oregon, 1988. In ERIC, ED299567.

> This report describes analytic assessment of student writing based on six areas: ideas and content; organization and development; voice; word choice; sentence structure; and the conventions of writing. Writing samples and scores for each grade level are included.

Anecdotal Records

Rhodes, Lynn K. and Sally Natenson-Mejia. "Anectdotal Records: A Powerful Tool for Ongoing Literacy Assessment." *The Reading Teacher* 45, 7 (September 1990): 44–48.

> The authors discuss anecdotal notes: how to collect and analyze them. Teachers reported that they saw and heard with greater clarity when using anecdotal records.

Checklists

"Evaluation Checklist for Student Writing in Grades K–3, Ottawa County." Ottawa City, Ohio, Office of Education, 1988. In ERIC, ED299583.

> This checklist was the primary record-keeping tool for a competency-based education program in Ohio. Guidelines for the development of the checklist are included.

Conferences

Bloom, Diane. "Conferencing: Assessing Growth and Change in Student Writing." New Jersey State Department of Education, June 1986. In ERIC, ED308513.

> This booklet presents three practical procedures for conferencing to help upper elementary level teachers evaluate the language development of students as they teach the writing process.

Goldstein, Lynn M. and Susan Conrad. "Student Input and Negotiation of Meaning in ESL Writing Conferences." *TESOL Quarterly* 24, 3 (Fall 1990): 443–460.

This article examines the degree of student control in writing conferences when English is the second language of the student. It focuses particularly on how students dealt with revision.

Turbill, Jan, ed. *No Better Way to Teach Writing.* Rozelle, New S. Wales, Australia, 1982.

This book describes the conference approach to teaching writing as it is practiced in an Australian Writing Project. It is divided into grade-level sections (K–2; primary) and contains a chapter on evaluation.

Valcourt, Gladys. "Inviting Rewriting: How to Respond to a First Draft." *Canadian Journal of English Language Arts* 12, 1–2: 29–36.

This article examines teachers' responses to students' first drafts. It suggests three ways to encourage rewriting: dialog feedback, student conferences, and reader-reaction summaries.

Vukelich, Carol and LuAnn Laverson. "Text Revisions by Two Young Writers Following Teacher/Student Conferences." *Journal of Research in Childhood Education* 3, 1 (Spring-Summer 1988): 46–54.

This article describes ways in which two second-grade writers used questions and comments made by their teacher during revising conferences.

Contracts

Beale, Walter and Don King. "A Grading Contract that Works." *Exercise Exchange* 26, 1 (Fall 1981): 17–20.

This article describes a contract the authors developed for freshman English. It could be adapted, however.

Holistic Measures

Gearhart, Maryl, et. al. "Writing Portfolios at the Elementary Level: A Study of Methods for Writing Assessment." In ERIC, ED344900 (1992).

This study investigated the utility and meaningfulness of using holistic and analytic scoring rubrics for portfolios.

Herron, Jeannine. "Computer Writing Labs: A New Vision for Elementary Writing." *Writing Notebook: Creative Word Processing in the Classroom* 9, 3 (January 1992): 31–33.

This article asserts that writing must have as honored a place as reading in first grade instruction. It discusses the need for computers, cooperative learning, and holistic assessment. It reports on implementation in a Los Altos, CA, school.

Myers, Miles. *A Procedure for Writing Assessment and Holistic Scoring.* Urbana, IL: National Council of Teachers of English, 1980.

This explanation for holistic scoring has been used by many school districts for district-wide writing assessments, such as writing proficiency tests, for over ten years. It is considered a classic in the field.

Vaac, Nancy Nesbitt. "Writing Evaluation: Examining Four Teachers' Holistic and Analytic Scores." *Elementary School Journal* 90, 1 (September 1989): 87–95.

This study examines the concurrent validity of holistic scores and analytic ratings of the same writing samples.

Portfolios

Cooper, Winfield. "What is a Portfolio?" *Portfolio News,* Spring 1991.

This essay offers a collection of twelve definitions of what portfolios are, drawn from a variety of teachers and schools.

Hanson, Jane. "Literacy Portfolios." *The Reading Teacher* 45, 8 (April 1992): 604.

This article discusses New Hampshire's reevaluation of its literacy portfolio system. Researchers found that students are better able to determine their own abilities and progress.

"Picture of a Portfolio." *Instructor* 101, 7 (March 1992): 26–28.

This article summarizes the Vermont Department of Education's portfolio system for grades 4, 8, and 12. It offers examples from a fourth-grade portfolio.

Portfolio News. A quarterly published by the Portfolio Assessment Clearinghouse. Winfield Cooper and Jon Davies, co-directors. c/o San Dieguito Union High School District, 710 Encinitas Boulevard, Encintas, CA 92024.

This quarterly is published fall, winter, spring, and summer. It includes brief articles on the uses of portfolios in different content areas as well as in different parts of the country.

Vermont Department of Education. "A Different Way of Looking at Math: Explaining Portfolios to Students." *Portfolio News,* Winter 1991.

This article explains how portfolios were used in math for fourth and eighth graders. A definition and rationale are given.

Vermont Department of Education. "Explaining Portfolios to Students in Vermont, Part II: Writing 'Your History as a Writer.'" *Portfolio News,* Winter 1992.

This article discusses the what, why, and how to portfolio keeping as it is used in Vermont.

"Writing and Reading Portfolios in Primary Grades." *Portfolio News,* Winter 1992.

This article reviews Donald Graves' book *Build a Literate Classroom* from a portfolio perspective. It includes details of creating portfolios from work folders by selection, replacement, and addition.

Primary-Trait Scoring

Bebermeyer, Ruth, et al. "Sample Exercises and Scoring Guides." ERIC, November 30, 1982 (ED224036).

This paper presents forty writing assignments and sixteen primary-trait scoring guides used by elementary and secondary teachers who participated in a writing research project.

Holdzkom, David, et al. "Purpose and Audience in Writing: A Study of Uses of the Primary-Trait System in Writing Instruction." Paper presented at the annual conference of the American Educational Research Association, Montreal, April 1983. In ERIC, ED236687.

> This study investigated instructional uses of primary-trait scoring techniques devised by the National Assessment of Educational Progress. Eleven elementary and secondary teachers participated in the study. The scoring techniques were used for five specified purposes.

Student-Centered Strategies

Collins, Jeffrey. "Establishing Peer Evaluation of Writing: Students Need an Informed Teacher Model." In ERIC, ED243122 (1983): 11 pages.

> The author of this essay argues that peer evaluation promotes ownership of writing and that the key to the success of peer evaluation is teacher modeling in conferences. The teacher encourages the students to respond to each other as real readers would.

Jochum, Julie. "Whole-Language Writing: The Critical Response." *Highlights* (the Journal of the Minnesota Reading Association) 11, 2 (May 1989): 5–7.

> This article discusses peer response to writing. Writers' circles, writers' conferences, and the writer as informant to open-ended questions are discussed.

Lewis, Melva and Arnold Lindaman. "How Do We Evaluate Student Writing? One District's Answer." *Educational Leadership* 46, 7 (April 1989): 70.

> The district reported on in this article has the entire school write about one topic in the fall and then another in the spring. Students evaluate their own writing; parents and teachers offer comments.

Writing Process Strategies

Hillerich, Robert. *Teaching Children to Write K–8: A Complete Guide to Developing Writing Skills.* Englewood Cliffs, NJ: Prentice-Hall, 1985.

> This book has as its cornerstone the notion that children learn to write by writing in an enjoyable atmosphere. The last chapter deals with evaluating the writing process.

Proett, Jackie and Kent Gill. *The Writing Process in Action: A Handbook for Teachers.* Urbana, IL: National Council of Teachers of English, 1986.

> This brief but excellent handbook outlines the writing process and illustrates it with classroom activities. Evaluation strategies reviewed include traditional methods and holistic scoring methods.

Written Comments

Coleman, Mary. "Individualizing Instruction through Written Teacher Comments." *Language Arts* 57, 3 (March 1980): 294–298.

> This article suggests four ways of using written comments to communicate with individual students: reaction, encouragement, correction, and evaluation.

Corley, Donna. "Thoughts from Students of Language Arts at the Elementary, High School, and College Level on Teacher Written Comments." Paper presented at the annual meeting of the Southern Educational Research Association, Austin, Texas, January 25–27, 1990. In ERIC, ED316876.

This study was conducted to determine how written teacher comments affected students who received them. At the elementary level, all of the students read the comments. Sixty-six percent of the elementary students read the comments to see what they did wrong; the rest read them to see what they had done right.

Olson, Mary and Paul Raffeld. "Effects of Written Comments on the Quality of Student Composition and the Learning of Content." *Reading Psychology* 8, 4 (1987): 273–293.

This study investigated the effect of written teacher comments on students. The findings support the idea that content comments are helpful to students.

INDEX